Every Good Thing

Also by Cheryl Wilfong

Every Good Thing

Cheryl Wilfong

2013

Cheryl Wilfong
Heart Path Press, L3C
314 Partridge Road
Putney VT 05346

www.meditativegardener.com

ISBN: 978-0-9825664-5-9

Follow The Meditative Gardener *on Facebook*

My dear Friend,

Welcome to the 2013 edition of my writings. While most of these essays were written this year, some essays were written years ago. Sometimes it takes time for the purpose of a piece to gel and to articulate itself.

Thanks to my sister, Dona Fuller, for her comments on the memoir pieces. She also worked on several stories (mostly about our mother) that didn't make the cut, but might some other year, after they have come into focus.

As usual, the Warning Label reads:

WARNING

You may think you know the characters
in these writings, but if you ask the
people with those names, you'll hear a
completely different story.

Thanks to Mike Fleming, the editor of this volume, who kindly pushes me to write more deeply and more thoroughly. I remain grateful to Jan Frazier and her writing groups where the first drafts of most of these pieces were written. As always, deep affection and appreciation go to this book's designer, Carolyn Kasper.

Cheryl

cheryl.wilfong@gmail.com

Contents

TRAVEL 35

CHERYL'S MEMOIRS 59

DAD   85

HERE COMES TROUBLE   103

BEST OF THE BLOG 2013:
The Divine Emotions   115

THE SURPRISE
OF MY LIFE   129

CONCLUSION 143

BILL

Intermeshing Households

BILL AND I MET in middle age, when we each had a houseful of stuff. He moved into my house and paid me rent for the first several years. By and large, the furnishings remained mine because he was going through a prolonged, torturous divorce.

But he missed his house, and he missed owning a house. I toyed briefly with selling him half of my house, but my divorced parents unified on this subject: "Keep your house in your name." My father was absolutely vehement about keeping my house in my own name.

Over the years, Bill bought the improvements—hot-water baseboards, Duette accordion shades for the south-facing windows, oak flooring in the living room. Actually, the first improvement, which was paid for by his 86-year-old mother, was a new refrigerator.

I told him that in Native American societies the woman owned the tipi, and if she wanted a divorce, the man would come home to find his saddle outside the door. If I ever wanted to divorce him—even though we weren't married—he would come home and find his refrigerator outside the front door.

Twenty years later, I bought a new refrigerator, and Bill's refrigerator was taken away by Efficiency Vermont; I received a $50 check in the mail. What would I put outside the front door now? Maybe I've lost my chance.

Combining the households of two mature adults does have labyrinthine qualities. Bill has his own room—his music studio, his den—in the daylight basement, and in that room he can do anything he wants. His paintings and decor are in the brown-to-rust spectrum. Upstairs the living room is teal, the dining room purple, the kitchen pink, and my office shocking pink. The color we agreed on for the bedroom is light blue.

One of the places Bill has exerted his influence is in our mug collection. My blue mugs, flowered mugs, and oriental mugs sit on a shelf in a closet, while Bill's brown and tan mugs are the ones accessible for daily use.

In the intermeshing of households also comes the question of which friends do I/we/he keep? Early on, I let some friends go, because Bill didn't particularly like them. Some friends stopped inviting me over for dinner. When it came to visiting my extended family in Indiana, Bill finally, after ten or twelve years, just bailed out. I go; he doesn't.

Bill has his collection of musical friends: his voice teacher, Jim; his clarinetist and biking friend, Karen; Leslie, the soprano who is so thrilled to sing duets with him that she kisses him when they part; Kathi, his flutist; and many others.

I have my collection of single women friends and Dharma friends.

Although people are accustomed to seeing Bill and me together, we don't act much like a duet. We each solo through our days, and often through our evenings as well. We have a few couple-friends whom we see once or twice a year. Intermeshing our couple-friends has been about as successful as intermeshing our mug collection. Some we see; some we don't. The people who love me don't necessarily love or even like Bill; the people who love Bill may feel they don't have anything in common with me.

The myth that two people become one is for the young. Even if Jesus said it (Mark 10:8), I do not believe it. I don't take these words on blind faith because they are not congruent with my experience. If I had to become Bill-ish, I would be furious all the time. If he had to become more Cheryl-ish, well, he just couldn't do it. If I had to combine my checking account with his, we would argue over money at least once a week. With our separate checking accounts, he tries to be generous to me, and I try to be generous to him.

For the middle-aged who have tried out those myths about love and found them lacking, there is the glorious interdependence of independent lives. Ahhh.

Sailing in the Caribbean

BILL WENT ON A yoga and sailing cruise in the British Virgin Islands for his 77th birthday. He likes to sail and has wanted to sail in the Caribbean for years—decades, really. He's heard other men in his Rotary Club talk about going sailing in the Virgin Islands, so it's been on his bucket list.

Neither sailing nor the Caribbean is on my bucket list, so I stayed home. While I'm away from home on retreat for eight weeks a year, Bill keeps the home fires burning. So it was my turn to long for his companionship while he was far away.

I look forward to being at home alone, something that hasn't happened since Bill moved in 23 years ago. My birthday present to him is that I paid for his airplane ticket, and I also drove him to Logan Airport on Saturday, November 10, and was planning to pick him up on Saturday, November 17. I wrapped up little birthday surprises and sneaked them into his suitcase when he wasn't looking.

I really enjoyed thinking about how I could support Bill in doing something he's always wanted to do, until I received an e-mail from a friend. She and her husband are going on a Caribbean cruise with her sister to celebrate her sister's 65th birthday. I imagined this foursome living the beautiful life in a luxurious cabin aboard a big cruise ship, drinking wine with every dinner, calling at a different island port every day, shopping and shopping.

And suddenly I felt guilty. I shouldn't send Bill off alone for his birthday. Well, not alone exactly; he was going with a dozen other yoga enthusiasts from Core Flow Yoga in West Brattleboro. Maybe I should go with him? Even though I don't want to?

What my friend is doing is what people are *supposed* to do—celebrate a loved one's birthday by going on a cruise with them. However, I am not only uninterested in sailing and the Caribbean, I also hope I never go on another cruise. I don't want to go island hopping or island shopping, and I don't want to sit under palm trees or on a sailboat drinking piña coladas or margaritas. If that's the beautiful life, I have no desire for it. I would rather stay home.

I am so happy for Bill. But I don't feel happy for my friend and her sister, and that's probably why I'm feeling unhappy with myself. Maybe it's time to wish that foursome *buen viaje, bon voyage* as they sail into the sunset so I can have the peace of solitude.

Separate Vacations

BILL AND I TOOK separate vacations in November 2012. I could say "for the first time in 24 years," but that's not quite accurate. I have gone away—mostly on retreat or to see my family in Indiana—and left Bill at home for eight or ten weeks every year. But this was the time that Bill left me home alone for a whole week.

I rather love reverting to my native schedule. Wake up at 4:00, make the bed (this is something I learned from Bill), get dressed, meditate, and write. If Bill's not in bed, I'm not tempted to go back for a nap.

One morning I did a two-hour project that I had been thinking about for a year. Wow! That felt good.

I also love the opportunity to declutter. The kitchen table is clean. Bill usually keeps a stack of mail and papers to read just on the left side of his place. Sometimes I set his bowl of chili right on top of his scattered paper. My two-thirds of the table is cleared off, but my paper pile is very nearby, so I'm not guiltless on this score.

The houseplants are watered and trimmed. I've taken cuttings of straggly begonias and geraniums. I've had time to watch webinars on The Compassionate Brain as well as *Tricycle* magazine's Buddhist movie of the month. I'm even straightening up the disaster area of my office.

I think of these separate vacations as a way of practicing

for each other's death. One day, one of us will be home alone, eating what we want without the clutter of the other person's eating habits obstructing our view of the inside of the refrigerator. One day, we will be sleeping alone in a big bed. One day, we will be walking into an empty house every day, day after day.

To my surprise, Bill called me from his sailboat in the Caribbean on Sunday night. He was using the captain's cell phone and was sitting around on deck under a starry sky, having just finished a dinner of roasted shrimp.

Oh, my dear Bill. Such a beautiful location. I could almost feel a warm tropical breeze coming through the wireless phone. So relaxing. Yoga on the beach with one teacher instructing and the other gently adjusting everyone's postures. Sailing a 42-foot boat and sleeping in a closet of a cabin after gallantly donating his assigned cabin in the bow to the yoga teacher and her mother.

Bill was so happy. Is there anything more delicious than knowing that your nearest and dearest is very happy? Happy even though they are 2,000 miles away from you.

Yoga Partners

I JUST REALIZED, WHEN BILL and I were in yoga class together, as we have been for the past seven years, that we were the only couple there. Bill is the only man in yoga, except for the teacher, Scott, a big man who was a quarterback in high school. Yoga is something Bill and I do together on Wednesday evenings.

In March, Bill and I went on a yoga vacation in the Yucatán, offered by a local yoga teacher. Bill was ready for a break from winter, and I, having just been in Southeast Asia for six weeks, was ready to be with Bill.

Bill loves the Caribbean, and for his 77th birthday in November I sent him on a yoga yacht tour of the British Virgin Islands. Every morning a dozen people, mostly young and a few young-at-heart, jumped off the sailboat, swam to shore, did yoga on the beach, and then swam back to the boat for a day of sailing. Bill is a sailor and a swimmer. I am not. He also drinks, and drinking is de rigueur in the Caribbean. I do not drink.

He had a great time sailing the 42-foot boat with the captain and, on their only beach day, learning to sail a Hobie Cat.[1] He loved looking at the beautiful young bodies

---

1. A Hobie Cat is a two-person catamaran.

on the companion sailboat, who spent more time drinking and mating than doing yoga.

Still, I was surprised when I threw out the bait of yoga in the Yucatán three months later, and he bit. He was the only man in our group of fourteen aging-but-fit women. We spent two hours doing yoga on the beach every morning before our tropical Mexican breakfast. Then we were free for the rest of the day.

This year (the fourteenth year of this yoga program), the group was very inclusive. If Bill didn't want to do an activity, like take a walking tour of Puerto Morelos, I could find a woman or three to go with. When I didn't want to go snorkeling in a *cenote*, he went along with four other women.[2] Often, the whole group went to the same restaurant for dinner. No one was excluded.

At our closing group dinner, Bill received the "Hombre Award" for braving the menopausal majority.

Bill does yoga every day at home for his back. Sometimes, I ask him to let me know when he's doing it, so that I can join him. I feel deep gratitude to be doing yoga with dear Bill.

But please, no partner exercises.

2.　A *cenote* is a sinkhole in the limestone, often 100 to 200 or more feet deep, with a deep pool of water at the bottom.

Terminal Cases

"We are all terminal cases."

The World According to Garp

OUR NINE-YEAR-OLD CITY GRANDSON, Max, is going to an Outdoor Skills Camp in Boston, where he's learning kayaking, canoeing, and rock climbing. He loves the rock climbing.

I remember him as a one-year-old climbing to the top of the coffee table and onto the back of the sofa, where many tumbles were taken, so I've been waiting for his rock-climbing phase. The thought of a loved one on a sheer face of rock is enough to put my heart in my throat.

A monk cleaning the room of the Thai Forest master Ajahn Chah asked him why he had such a beautiful cup. After all, monks are ascetics with very few possessions. Ajahn Chah replied, "I see the cup as already broken."

If I took Ajahn Chah's advice and really believed that we are all terminal cases, how would I respond from my heart?

In July, Bill took me up to the White Mountains. We hiked 1.6 miles to Lonesome Lake, where there's an Appalachian Mountain Club hut. The next day we hiked 2.4 miles up the granite dome of Cannon Mountain and then back down to Lonesome Lake. If I were being dramatic, I would say that Bill dragged me to the mountains and hauled me straight up boulder-strewn Cannon Mountain.

When we arrived at the observation platform on top, we had a glorious 360-degree view. I shed my wool socks and hiking boots and collapsed onto a bench. Then people in flip-flops arrived, overweight people arrived, and a woman carrying her large purse. They had all come up on a ten-minute gondola ride. They didn't need two quarts of water, hiking poles, and a large stash of protein and energy bars. The next day their knees were not complaining every time they took a step up or a step down. A staircase didn't elicit involuntary groans from them.

Instead, I remind myself that my beloved Bill is a terminal case. And this body, too, will soon enough be broken.

So I keep the complaining thoughts at bay and focus instead on the great good fortune to have someone who is so interested in exercising my body that he'll haul me to the mountains and drag me along behind him as we climb a ladder up a sheer granite face where, someday, our grandson Max will be hiking himself.

CHERYL

Wrinkly Pix

I WENT TO WALGREEN'S ON January 10 to have passport pictures taken, although not for a passport. My passport finally came home on January 9 after being shuffled in large stacks of paper at the Myanmar Embassy in Washington, D.C., for more than three weeks. Whew— home at last! Safe within my grasp. Let's just pray it stays there for the next six weeks while I'm in Southeast Asia.

The so-called passport photos are for a visa to Laos, where I arrive on February 1, to be shuffled and stacked in less than half an hour *if* I'm at the head of the line getting off the airplane from Yangon.

The Walgreen photo-taker put the camera chip into the computer there at the photo counter and—*voilà!*—I could see my face in full wrinkly color. She arranged all those smiling wrinkles so they fit into the bull's-eye target of the computer screen.

Wow! I look old. I mean o-l-d. How did I get this old? I try not to look at this conundrum too closely most days, but there it was, staring me in the face.

I really do not understand how someone that age can go get into her car, throw those wrinkly pix into the back seat, drive off to the circus school, pull herself onto a trapeze, stand on the bar, and balance on one foot.

∨ The Pretzel

I WALKED OUT OF SAM'S Army Navy Store one January afternoon and bumped into Melissa, my trapeze teacher. Before I knew her name, back when Bill and I simply attended performances at the New England Center for Circus Arts three or four times a year, I called her The Pretzel.

The Pretzel has extreme flexibility. She can do a handstand and touch her toes to her head—even though Melissa-the-Pretzel is 30 years old, she has the build of a thirteen-year-old and weighs about 85 pounds soaking wet, which she often is, from the perspiration of juggling on a tightrope or springing into a somersault in the air to land on someone's shoulders. She can stand on the head of a strong man and then squat down there. She can do the over-splits and splits upside down. And, of course, she can do all sorts of static trapeze and flying trapeze tricks.

I bumped into her on the sidewalk outside Sam's and she said, "I'm flying to Australia tomorrow. I have a one-month audition with the best aerial troupe in Australia. If it works out, I'll be there for two years."

"Wow!" I said. "That's wonderful. And you're not too old? I mean, you're young, but for this work, you're old."

"No," she said. "They want someone with good communication skills."

"Great," I said. "Maybe we'll come visit you. I'll keep my eye on your Facebook page."

"I've got to run," she said.

We hugged. "Thanks for teaching me trapeze. And I love you."

She dashed off.

Sometimes I wonder if guardian spirits are arranging these sorts of encounters. The Pretzel could have just disappeared from my life, but I had the opportunity to express my deep gratitude directly to her, whether or not I ever see her again in my life.

The Disappearance of Cursive

I READ IN THE NEWS that most high school students cannot read cursive. They learn it in third grade and then don't use it, so they've forgotten it by the time they have to write an essay in cursive for the SAT.

In other words, all my journals are going to be indecipherable hieroglyphics in just a few years. If nobody can read them, why not just throw them out in the trash? Or if you live in Vermont, use them to start the kindling in the wood stove?

Because I see my grandchildren, who are nine and twelve, just a few times a year, one friend encourages me to write them weekly postcards. Sometimes I remember to write; often I forget.

But now I'm reinvigorated. I'm writing postcards to teach them to read cursive. I write carefully and as beautifully as I can with short sentences so they won't lose interest. I see my role more clearly. Writing, the literal pen-to-paper handwriting, is about to disappear from our culture. Only the printed word and the hand-printed word will remain.

Ubuntu Means Interconnected

M Y DHARMA FRIEND DEBBY recently returned from a three-week retreat in South Africa followed by a three-week game tour to several national parks. The name of the game tour was Ubuntu. Debby explained that *ubuntu* means something like "I exist because you exist." *Ubuntu* refers to our interconnectedness and reminds us that we each belong to a greater whole. As it turned out, the very next day, Sunday, was *ubuntu*-day for me.

I was giving a Dharma talk at Northampton Insight that night, and so had prepared a PowerPoint slide show on my recent retreat in Burma. One of my travel companions sent me several of her photos. I borrowed a projector from another Dharma friend, but couldn't get my laptop to communicate with it.

At 4:00 p.m. I called my neighbor Connie about borrowing her laptop. "Come on down," she said. I took all my hardware to her house, and within fifteen minutes she showed me the proper connections.

Then I drove south and got twenty minutes away from home before I realized that I had forgotten to bring an extension cord. I called David, who lives in town. At that moment he was working as production manager for the afternoon show of the aerial circus show, so he asked Jerry, whom he was standing next to, if I could borrow an extension cord from the New England Youth Theatre (NEYT). By the time I pulled into NEYT, Jerry was just driving into the parking lot himself. Two minutes later, I stowed a 50-foot extension cord with an electrical box of four outlets in my car.

While asking for help comes easily for some people, I've spent most of my life acting as if I'm self-reliant. I'm a do-it-yourselfer from way back. I'm even slightly scared of people, but really, you know, it is possible to ask anyone for anything. After all, we are all *ubuntu*, interconnected.

Thanks to six friends, I was able to connect my PowerPoint to the projector. As we like to say in our neighborhood, "It takes a village to . . ." give a PowerPoint.

The Sleep of the Old

EVEN BEFORE HOT FLASHES, I stuck my feet outside the covers. This is the way I go to sleep, even in midwinter—with my feet sticking out of the blankets.

Sometimes Bill covers up my feet when he comes to bed an hour later, but by the time he's read a few pages, my feet will have found their way outside the covers again, even though I'm asleep. Bill can't figure this out since he sometimes takes naps or even has sex with his socks on. It makes him chilly just to look at my uncovered feet.

Several years ago, I realized that cold feet delay the onset of restless legs. Since restless legs begin when the body is relaxed, sleeping with my feet sticking out of the covers has the additional advantage of allowing me to drop off to sleep without an attack of restless legs.

When Bill and I were planning to hike the Haleakala Crater in Maui a few years ago we bought summer-weight sleeping bags, but then, since it occasionally snows up there at 8–10,000 feet, I also bought liners that would add another five or ten degrees of warmth to the usability of the sleeping bags. We didn't end up using the liners, though, because the cabin we stayed in kept us warm enough. But the liners seemed a perfect thing to take to the Appalachian Mountain Club hut, which advises you to bring your own sheet and pillowcase. They supply the wool blankets.

The evening at Lonesome Lake was warm even at 1,600 feet. I went to dinner in shorts. By the time the sun sank below the mountaintops and set on the cloudless, star-filled night, though, the liner felt good. For about two minutes. Then I wanted to stick my feet out of the liner bag but couldn't, so I lay still, willing myself to coolness. Outside, hiking boots clumped down the boardwalk to the Clivus Multrum outhouse. I read a book on my iPad. Two hours after lights-out at 9:30, I was, unusually, still wide awake. I might as well visit Clivus again. If only I had a Swiss Army knife! But that handy tool had been put aside in September 2001, when we could no longer travel with sharps, and it has surfaced only rarely since then.

Finally, I was desperate enough to think of my gum stimulator, an implement with a rubber tip. Using its metal handle, I poked a hole in the bottom of my light jersey sleeping bag liner. I carefully ripped an eight-inch hole, settled back in, stuck my feet out and immediately fell asleep.

"How did you sleep?" people asked at breakfast the next morning.

"I slept the sleep of the old," I said. "I got up to pee five times." I didn't go into the other details. Gray-heads already know the territory. We're all snoring and waking up parched. Our mouths are dry, and we are dehydrated. When we pinch the skin on the backs of our hands, it sticks together and takes a few seconds to flatten out again. Dry mouth leads to gum disease, so not only is snoring not good for your respiratory system, it's not good for your teeth and gums, either. That's why I have a gum stimulator for my aging gums. That handy, handy implement.

IN THE GARDEN

Ode to My GardenWay Cart

IN APRIL I'M INEXTRICABLY joined to my GardenWay cart. It goes everywhere I go. Or maybe I go
everywhere it goes.

Assuming April begins snowless—and that *is* an
assumption, since some years the snow cover persists
until mid-month—I drive my truck to get a load of bunny
manure. Vermont's extra season, mud season, lies between
winter and spring and prevents me from driving anywhere
close to my flower beds. I can still see the tire ruts of past
laziness indented in the lawn.

Here's where the GardenWay cart comes in. I rake it
full of bunny poop and begin shoveling the soft brown pel-
lets onto the dooryard garden–my white garden. After two
or three cartloads there, I work my way downhill: the bulb
garden, the patio garden, the hosta bed under one old apple
tree, my wildflower bed under another old apple. Behind
the house lies the herb garden, then the east hillside and the
edge of the yard. By this time I've worked my way out to the
"meadow" that Bill cleared when he first moved in, thereby
doubling the size of the lawn. I don't touch my moss garden,
carefully trying to maintain the green carpet that used to lie
among pine trees but is now out in the open. I've worked
my way around the edge of Bill's meadow, annexing a bit

more of it each year until now it's edged with flower beds and shrubs.

By this time I've hauled five truckloads of bunny manure, and I haven't even gotten to the vegetable garden and my cutting beds.

Next, it's time to lay new wood chips on the paths. Last year's chips have degraded and dandelions have jumped feet-first into the paths despite the fact that their roots have to push their way through the landscaping fabric that underlies the path of chips.

My wood chip inventory was delivered last fall by the tree service—$25 for a huge heap. Each GardenWay cart-load covers about ten feet. That translates into 30 loads, but I just count up to three, then quit and change the pace. Later or next day, I cart three more loads.

This year I had the bark mulch delivered—fourteen cubic yards of double-processed pine bark. One dump-truck load equals nine of my pickup truck loads. I justify the big expenditure by figuring that I just saved myself nearly nine hours of commuting time to pick it up myself. Yes, $420 is a lot of money, but I have a lot of gardens to cover.

The only work left for my truck is a load or two of peat moss to mulch the cutting beds of annuals and the new perennial beds that aren't totally planted yet. I'm still building up a memorial garden in honor of Bill's mother, Mabel. And I'm just beginning a blue garden. Blue—my favorite color. Yes. I've decided I need a blue garden.

"What a lot of work," say many visitors to my gardens.

"What a lot of play," I smile back to them. This is my idea of a playground: exercising big muscle groups early in the season with the aid of my GardenWay cart. By the time May and its budding trees unfold I can begin to focus on finer motor coordination. I dig up, divide, and transplant. I edge the beds. I haul buckets of compost to the plants and buckets of dead foliage and the finally-fallen-off beech leaves to the compost pile. As spring fades to summer, I can focus on really fine motor skills like picking single tufts of grass out of the moss garden.

When the hauling work—the horse work, I call it—of April is done, the work of maintenance, then I can start to dream and play around in the garden again. I can begin to paint with flowers, to plant pale lavender iris next to pale yellow, and move that bright yellow daylily out of the pink-and-white bed.

During July and August, the GardenWay cart only takes an occasional walk, every other day or so. It spends most of the summer in the garage, protecting itself from too much exposure to the sun. Then, in the fall, I fill it full of dead flowers and dying stalks. "If it's brown, I'll cut it down. If it's green, it's clean." I cart the dead plant bodies to the compost pile, then store the GardenWay cart in the basement for its well-deserved winter rest.

The Bottom of the Compost Pile

I COME TO THE BOTTOM of one compost pile in early May. I love the excavation, perhaps because I wanted to be an archaeologist when I was eleven.

I find desiccated bones (chicken). Yes, I know you're not supposed to put animal products in a compost pile, but sometimes I do it anyway. Nowadays I cremate bones and bacon grease in my wood stove.

In addition to the chicken bones, I find the bamboo plates from my neighbors' daughter's wedding, three summers ago. The bamboo plates are technically biodegradable, but they're still completely recognizable. The plastic cups made from corn now look like splintered plastic. I sort those out and put them into the trash. I'm not counting on their biodegradability.

Food for the wedding was catered by the Top of the Hill Grill barbeque place. No wonder I'm finding so many rib bones.

I wheelbarrow loads of compost to the vegetable garden and sprinkle bucketfuls on my former herb garden that I'm refurbishing as a flower-vegetable medley garden.

I pot up my extra plants. Really, this is the main reason I garden: so that I can give plants away.

I pot up plants for the Perennial Swappers who meet every two weeks, for the Brattleboro Garden Club plant sale on Memorial Day weekend, and for the Putney Library plant sale in early June. Every Saturday morning, I scavenge free flowerpots at the Swap Shop at the landfill. I recycle every yogurt container, hummus container, and to-go box, and reuse them for potting up little plants.

I dig up and divide the biggest clumps of gone-by daffodils. These require medium-size pots and several handfuls of compost in each one. As I paw through the compost, I toss the desiccated bones into the woods behind the compost bins. After a number of years, the soil around the bins has become quite dark and rich, too.

When I reach the bottom of the compost pile, I drive the truck to Mail-Rite to pick up some new pallets and reconstruct the old bins whose pallet sides look like decayed teeth. I tie the new pallets together at the corners and lay down a black plastic floor to prevent tree roots from sucking up the compost from the bottom.

Then I toss in the latest offerings: dead daffodils and coffee grounds still in their Melitta brown-paper filter, orange and grapefruit rinds, banana peels, and—well, I can't help myself—a few fish bones.

Nancy's Lawn

WHEN I GO TO writing group on Tuesday mornings, I love to park on Nancy's lawn because it's so convenient, and it's flat. Chances are, since I'm running late, that the parking lot is already full, and getting into that back corner is awkward. I could park behind (or is that in front of?) someone else, but that seems improper, as if there's a handbook of parking etiquette that Emily Hitching-Post has written.

More likely, I've been trained by experience. People need to leave early and ask you to please move your car. Or they want to leave late, and they're boxing you in. You sit in your car for a minute or two thinking, *Surely, they won't be much longer.* At minute three, you heave a big sigh, shove your car door open, and drag yourself back into your host's home. You smile brightly, "Could the blue Prius that's parked behind me please move?"

You're polite. They're polite. You're bothered. They're bothered.

"Oh, sure," they say and spring to the door, keys in hand. Or they finish that last bit of delicious conversation and come out to their car one or two minutes later.

You're already in your driver's seat, both hands gripping the wheel, and you're breathing huffy little out-breaths as you tell yourself how ridiculous you are. Or you look at your watch and think, *Okay, I'm going to be five minutes late. Now just relax.* And you sigh out a longer, deeper breath, as if that will change the state of affairs.

I'm never going to put myself in that situation again, you think.

This is probably why, when I have a potluck, no one, I repeat no one, parks in any of the four spots in the driveway. Bill and I have our cars tucked neatly in the garage. We, the hosts, are not leaving or going anywhere. *Please* park behind us. But people don't even drive in the driveway. They park in the field that Bills mows every two weeks so that it looks green and pristine. They park on the side of my neighbor's driveway. Hmm. I haven't really quizzed the neighbors about how they feel about that.

At winter solstice, people park ten feet away from the bonfire pile. *Hmm,* I think, *don't you remember there's going to be a twelve-foot-tall flame right beside your car? Do you want your car to catch on fire?* I politely ask them to move. "There's going to be a big fire right beside your car. Do you think your car will be safe? All those hemlock branches in the pile send up a lot of sparks."

They move their car. I've learned to blockade that prime parking spot with luminarias. I certainly hope that no one will drive over a candle in a bag of sand and set their car on fire from below.

So I've learned not even to drive into Nancy's driveway. I park at the entrance. I run over dame's rocket, yarrow, and daisies, sacrificed in the name of making an easy getaway.

When you've gotta go, you've gotta go.

TRAVEL

Giving Up

THE FLIGHT FROM HARTFORD to Dallas–Fort Worth was uneventful. I did find a man sitting in "my" seat: 19F. He pointed to the man in front of him and said, "I had 18F." Then, with a silent glance, he pointed to 18A—an empty window seat. I understood this wordless exchange and pitched my day pack into the window seat. Really, I wasn't wedded to 19F. I just prefer a window seat.

I had an hour-plus layover at the sprawling DFW airport, where you take the "Skytrain" to get from one gate to another. I was just settling into my seat at Gate A25 when I heard my name called. I went to the desk and the gate check attendant asked if I would change seats so a couple could sit together. Their seat was farther back in the plane. Oh, well. I exchanged 19A for 27A.

I know that American Airlines is very picky about their "two carry-ons" rule, so I had already stuffed my pocketbook into my day pack. My roller bag is an unusual soft, blue-canvas backpack model with a tiny zip-on day pack that bulges out. The same gate-check attendant nabbed me, "Will that fit in the sizer?" She pointed to the open metal quadrangle. I already knew that it wouldn't. "We have to gate-check that," she said.

"But," I pleaded, "I can just unzip this little pack and stuff it on top, and it doesn't take any more room."

"Then you'll have three carry-ons. Thank you for understanding. Here's your receipt." She just kept talking so I didn't have a chance for a comeback, and I reluctantly took the gate-check receipt.

Well, at least I didn't have to pay $25 to check a bag, I thought. But I wasn't really consoled. I'd given up my seat to her, and now I had to give up my bag to her, too. It didn't seem fair.

As I walked to the end of the jet bridge, I heard a uniform say something to the flight attendants, "It shouldn't take too long." As he walked toward me, I could read his badge: "Union Pilot." *Oh-oh.* The pilot getting off the plane as we were getting on seemed like a farce.

I took my 27A seat and then watched as an Indian woman pleaded with the man in front of me to trade seats with her ten-year-old daughter who was sitting in 7E. He shook his head.

"I'll trade," I said. He can have my window seat, and I'll take your daughter's seat." I headed upstream, against the flow of passengers, to 7E. A rotund man in 7D on the aisle said, "She's crying, poor thing."

I squeezed into 7E—a bulkhead seat. The flight attendant who was attending to this transfer said, "Please place your day pack under your seat."

I did, and within a minute, I could feel my day pack being pushed against my heels. Another minute of pushing, pushing, push-sh-sh-ing, and the man in 8F spoke to me between the seats. "Please move your bag."

First my carry-on had been removed. Then I had removed. And now I was being asked to part with the only other thing I had—my day pack, which I refer to as my entertainment center. It contains a book, my Kindle, my knitting, sudoku, a stack of newsletters that had built up since my last flight five months ago, water, various snacks, socks in case my feet get cold, and a sweater in case my arms get cold. I removed a book and put my bag in the overhead bin.

I pluffed back down in my seat, and said to my rotund neighbor, whose right arm overflowed into "my" space, "I just want to cry."

The plane, fully loaded, continued to sit on the tarmac. The captain's voice came over the intercom. "We're just waiting for some paperwork to be signed off."

I sat in my seat and felt the pain around my heart, and I thought about how unfair it all was. Even after I'd given up my seat twice, and given up my bag *and* my day pack, nobody had given me anything. Not an inch. I closed my eyes. Tears trickled down my cheeks. The plane didn't move. My neighbor had exchanged a quietly crying ten-year-old girl for a quietly crying 64-year-old girl.

One of my meditation teachers says "Express your care and concern for your loved one, without expecting anything in return." I had been generous with my seats four times this morning. I had given up my luggage, piece by piece, and what had anyone given me? What would it be like to "expect nothing in return"?

Twenty minutes later we heard from the captain again. "It's getting too hot in the plane. We're going to ask you to de-plane."

So we all "de-planed" from our 737, and once again we were sitting in the waiting area at Gate A25. The announcement over the PA system was a way of saying that the metal cans of airplanes heat up fast in mid-July days at DFW.

An hour later, we reboarded our plane as though following a well-rehearsed drill. The plane backed up from the Jetway. And there it sat. The captain's voice came over the intercom. "A light that's supposed to go on has turned off. We need to return to the gate for maintenance."

We pulled into another gate; we deplaned; and people in the waiting area began bad-mouthing American Airlines. Half an hour later, the PA system told us to move to another gate and another airplane. On my way, I stopped at Auntie Anne's and bought a pack of cinnamon sugar twists. They were way off my diet, but I was seeking solace. After eating two cinnamon-sugar toast-like things, I felt much better and tossed the remaining four into the trash.

At two o'clock we began boarding amid warnings from the gate attendants: "The flight crew is going to time-out if we wait any longer, so please hurry on to the plane and sit down, so we can close the door." The thought of waiting for a new crew to arrive was too terrible to consider.

As I walked through first class, I asked one woman if she recognized everyone now. "Yes," she said. "It sort of feels like family."

I stashed my day pack into the overhead bin for the third time, and, nearly four hours late, the plane departed DFW.

I could judge those people who didn't want to trade their seats. I could have an opinion about the person sitting behind me who wanted my day pack out of "her" space. There's a verse in a chant that I aspire to. I'd like for my friends to sing it to me when I am on my deathbed:

Those who are friendly, indifferent, or hostile,
may all beings receive the blessings of my life.

Could I practice this well-wishing right now toward the beings who were indifferent to my needs and feelings, who were so invested in defining "their" space that they could not be generous? Could I wish that they would receive my generosity, and that I could find the peace to expect nothing, nothing in return?

$55 Flip-Flops

I LOVE GOING BAREFOOT BUT my feet are old, and plantar fasciitis kicks up in my heels after a week or so of padding around the house with no shoes on. I gave up wearing flip-flops twenty years ago, after I finally realized that the twinge in my right knee was flip-flop induced.

I gave away all my fun shoes and all my cute shoes and now wear only sensible shoes with orthotics in every single pair. One podiatrist frowned at my insistent wearing of Birkenstocks.

A winter visit to the chiropractor yielded her recommendation of Orthaheel shoes. I went to my local shoe store, and there on the shelf were flip-flops with a foot bed that looks like an orthotic. They were lavender! Of course I bought them for my trip to Southeast Asia. Well, yes, they cost $55. Sigh.

The good news is that I walked for six weeks in Southeast Asia in flip-flops (lavender!) with no twinges or pain. Then I took them with me to the Yucatán. A barefoot walk on the beach one morning induced a tiny twinge. *Hey—I thought walking barefoot on the sand was good for your feet!*

On went the foot-saving flip-flops. Worth every penny of that $55.

Money Laundering—
and Ironing

Y OU'VE HEARD OF MONEY laundering. One of my fellow travelers to Southeast Asia, Susan, became weary from ironing dollar bills.

If you've traveled to a Third World country, you know they like their U.S. currency crisp—without tears, folds, or marks. A couple of years ago in Belize, I bought some handcrafts from two ten-year-old girls who were distraught that the dollar bills I gave them were well worn. Our guide to the Mayan ruins shooed them away, but my heart still pings when I remember them.

In January, Connie, Susan, and I went to an emerging country, Burma, that operates on a cash economy—*no* ATMs. We could get a better exchange rate for crisp $100 bills dated after 2006. My bank had a few dozen hundred-dollar bills on hand, left over from the Christmas holidays. But Susan's bank had no hot-off-the-press U.S. currency, so she added her own heat. She ironed her $100 bills.

Expect the Unexpected

"**E**XPECT THE UNEXPECTED" IS the motto of the Experiment in International Living, where I met my traveling companions Connie and Susan 40 years ago.

But really, how do you feel when the unexpected clashes with the expected?

	Our Plan	What Actually Happened
leaving home	7:15 a.m.	7:40 a.m.
arriving at airport	8:45 a.m.	9:35 a.m.
plane departs	10:10 a.m.	10:35 a.m.
arrive at DC	11:40 a.m.	12:25 p.m.
depart for Tokyo	12:20 p.m.	The flight to Tokyo has already departed, so at 6:40 p.m.—after standing in three different customer-service lines—we decide to fly to San Francisco to avoid the snow that is forecast for the following morning, so we have an unplanned overnight layover in San Francisco in order to catch a flight to Tokyo at 11:10 a.m.—the next day.
arrive Bangkok	11:45 p.m.	11:45 p.m. The next day.

Life is happening, not always as we expected—or wanted. Yet, this is the way things are. Shall we fight against reality? Or shall we enjoy traveling and all our unexpected adventures?

Breakfast in Bangkok

MY SISTER TEASES MY Hoosier brother about the time he drove 2,000 miles to her home in Washington in my mother's old butterscotch-colored Oldsmobile, stayed for dinner, and flew home at 6:00 the next morning. I now have a story to top that: We flew to Bangkok for breakfast.

Arriving 24 hours later than expected, the taxi dropped us off at our friends' condo at 12:30 a.m. We talked until 2:00, went to bed, got up at 7:00, ate breakfast, and left at 10:45 a.m. for the airport. Ten hours at our friends place. At least we could lie down flat and stretch out in a bed. In the morning I opened their refrigerator and ate leftovers for breakfast (my favorite breakfast!).

Farewell, Bangkok.

Homestay in Yangon

WHEN WE ARRIVED IN Yangon, our friend Pwint was at the airport to meet us. She had brought her nephew, who hauled our big suitcases into a van and then drove us to Pwint's condo.

For the past few years, I have addressed Christmas cards to Pyay Gardens in Yangon, and now I got to see the address with my own eyes: three yellow, five-story buildings across the street from the Insein General Hospital. Later, I would simply tell taxi drivers "Insein Hospital."

Pwint lives by herself in her condo on the fifth floor, now that her husband has died of liver cancer. Her 30-year-old veterinarian son fled to the United States for asylum. Her daughter lives in Hong Kong. So Pwint was delighted to have company in her three-bedroom top-floor home. And we were delighted to have a homestay with a view of Aung San Suu Kyi's home on Inya Lake.

We parked those big suitcases and our thousands of dollars in crisp $100 bills. (There are no ATMs in Myanmar/Burma.) What a relief not to have to lug our queen-sized suitcases or a big wad of money everywhere during our two-week stay in Burma.

Using Pwint's as our home base, we packed our carry-on roller bags and flew off to Bagan for three days to see 40 square miles of tenth-century temples. Pwint was happy to see us when we arrived back at her home again, and she had yet another delicious Burmese dinner prepared for us.

In the mornings, we visited the nearby Thiri Mingalar market for breakfast groceries—yogurt sold in clay pots comes with tiny baggies of jaggery, a sort of thin molasses. Papaya, tangerines, three different varieties of bananas. Pwint also bought *mohinga*—the Burmese national breakfast—a dark broth of soup with a baggie of rice noodles to be added in just as you're ready to eat it.

We did our sight-seeing in the mornings and then, as the January afternoon temperature rose above 90, we retired to the swimming pool at a nearby hotel. The towel at the pool cost eight crisp dollar bills for the afternoon.

Pwint lives on the top floor of Building #1; her mother, Sanda, lives on the second floor of Building #2; and her sister-in-law, Cho, has a condo in Building #3.

Several times as we walked through the parking lot of the Pyay Gardens, we saw members of Pwint's extended family—her doctor niece just returning from an overnight shift or the nephew who had picked us up at the airport and who is studying engineering.

There we were, at home with family, 12,000 miles away from home.

Living History

FLYING ACROSS THE PACIFIC Ocean, on our way to Burma, Susan, Connie, and I were reading like fiends.

One advantage of traveling with two other people was that they brought different books than I did. As soon as I finished a book, I handed it off to them. Of course, when they finished a book, they offered it to me with a gleam in their eyes.

The three of us are of an age where we still deal in hard copy. What a relief to finally offload a thrice-read book at whatever hotel we stayed at, thereby making room in the suitcase for the newest silk scarves or cute little hand-woven bags from the market.

One of our favorite books was *Burma Surgeon* by Dr. Gordon Seagrave. He was a fourth-generation missionary in Burma. The previous three generations had lived in Rangoon (as Yangon was called by the British colonizers), so young Dr. Seagrave headed north to the frontier to establish his clinic and his family in the late 1920s.

There, near the Chinese border, he trained local women to be nurses; this involved learning their languages—Chin, Kachin, Karen, Karenni, Shan, Mon. (The Burmans are just the largest ethnic minority in this conglomerated country of Burma.)

In 1941, when the Japanese invaded Burma, Dr.

Seagrave was nearly 40. His wife and children evacuated to India. Dr. Seagrave and most of his nurses trudged west up and down steep mountains to escape the Japanese army and finally, after several weeks, crossed over into India. The tribal country of western India, called Nagaland or "Land of Serpents," was rugged and wild and not exactly welcoming. Seagrave and his nurses camped just a little east of there, in Assam, with General Joe Stilwell and a division of the U.S. Army. When the Americans and Chinese pushed back into Burma in 1943, Dr. Seagrave and his nurses accompanied them, setting up a new field hospital every two or three days as the front advanced.

Seagrave's autobiography of World War II is riveting. So we were thrilled to meet one of Dr. Seagrave's nurses— Pwint's elderly aunt, Nong.

Nong spoke English fluently, and she was a very engaging conversationalist. Her emotions played across her face as she told us about Dr. Seagrave and the war. The feelings of the war years still gripped her as tears came to her eyes, and we were entranced to hear living history from her lips.

Circular Train

ONE MORNING, AFTER PWINT and Connie had gone to the office, Susan and I took a taxi to the Central Train Station. We asked for the Circular Train and were directed to platform 7. A notice on the wall of a small ticket office on the platform read *Warmly Welcome & Take Care of Tourists.* I snickered, assuming that this is just another of the bad-English signs that one finds in foreign countries, but maybe it was actual dictation taken down from the dictator generals who run the country: no one has dared to change a word.

We went inside the office where three men were working, and the one behind a table directed us to sit down.

"One dollar," he said, and collected a single bill from each of us. (It was for just these occasions that Susan had ironed her bills.) Then he began to fill out a brief form. "Passport?" he asked. Of course, we were not carrying our passports with us, so he waved that question away, and asked for our passport numbers. I happened to have memorized mine, so I wrote it down, and Susan was amazed that I had that number at the tip of my mind. "I was a math major," I explain. "I can remember numbers."

He wrote out the ticket for "Cheryl Wilfong + 1," so Susan didn't need her number, after all.

A few minutes later the train rolled in, and we boarded a windowless, doorless car. What I mean is that the car was completely open-air. There were no doors in the spaces where doors would otherwise be, and there were no windows either. Once we started rolling, we could feel leaves of tree branches brushing the skin of the elbows we propped on the edge of our open window.

The mint-green molded plastic seats ran lengthwise down both sides of the car; they were in no way ergonomic. If you slouched back, the top rim hit you in exactly the wrong place in the middle of your back. Tall Susan sat erect, without benefit of any back support—at least to begin with. My short legs dangled above the floor, so I immediately did what everyone else was doing: I faced forward, crossing my legs on the seat in front of me, meditation-style.

This poky local train took three hours to complete its circle around Yangon. Local people got on and off. I couldn't see that any of them had a ticket. School-uniformed boys in white shirts and dark green *longyis*[3] clustered at the open door wearing their backpacks and probably daring each other to do what boys everywhere dare each other to do.

A man selling mandarin oranges walked through, and, through sign language, I bought four. An hour later a teenage girl and boy came by, selling corn on the cob boiled in the husk, and I bought one of them for my lunch. The sellers were ready to peel it for me, but I waved that service away with sign language, with the Third World food slogan

---

3 In Myanmar, both men and women wear long skirts called *longyis*, a two-meter length of cloth wrapped around the waist and tucked in on itself. (No belts.)

EVERY GOOD THING

loud in my mind: "If it's not boiled, cooked, or peeled, don't eat it." I'm sure these vendors have never seen the sign reading "Food service employees must wash their hands. . . ." Susan shook her head; she'd wait for a real restaurant.

One stop was especially lively—a market. Large trash bags full of fresh vegetables were hoisted onto the train through the open windows and piled in the wide middle aisle, so that the design of the lengthwise seats now made sense. The only way to walk through the car was to waddle over three-foot-tall bags stuffed with something or other.

I watched a young woman sitting next to me open a plastic grocery bag full of small green eggplants, cluster them in groups of six, and then band them together with twine made from dry husk.

We left behind the dusty shacks alongside the railroad and rolled through neat green gardens on one side and green fields on the other. I breathed deeply to feel such verdant spaciousness.

After a while, I began to look more frequently at the maps in the Lonely Planet guidebook and at Susan's watch. It seemed this trip must surely take five hours, but then, surprisingly, we arrived back at the Central Train Station. As advertised, the trip had taken just three hours.

Temple Pajamas

EVERY EVENING IN BURMA we went to a Buddhist temple, either the Shwe Dagon[4] or the Botataung[5]. By dark, most of the tourists had departed, and the temple became all-Burmese. One-year-olds learned to walk under the watchful eyes of hundreds of bronze Buddhas. Preschoolers ran around in what looked like pajamas.

Our friend Pwint explained that people don't sleep in pajamas in Burma, so kids might as well wear them for everyday clothes. PJs did look cool and comfortable. In fact, I bought some thin white cotton pajamas for meditating in Thailand, where it is customary for yogis to wear all white. Four weeks after leaving Burma, I was walking around a Thai temple in my white pajamas.

Sssshhhhh. Don't tell anyone that they're pajamas.

---

4 The Shwe Dagon is a great golden stupa, emblematic of Burma. It is, in a sense, their national cathedral, although it is all open-air.
5 The rebuilt Botataung is another landmark golden stupa in Yangon. Before the original pagoda was destroyed in World War II, it contained a relic of the Buddha.

EVERY GOOD THING

Chinese License Plates

IN LAOS I WISHED I could decipher the Laotian letters on the license plates, and then occasionally I would see blue license plates with Roman letters and Arabic numbers. These, it turned out, are cars from China, and the more I looked, the more blue license plates I saw.

The majority of tourists in Laos are Koreans, but most of them are on tour buses.

I was traveling with five neighbors, and we always hired a car and driver to take us from one place to another. Our neighbor Connie, who was there for work, and who speaks Lao, says Laos is the West Virginia of Southeast Asia. Six million people live in the mountains that the Ho Chi Minh Trail once ran through.

Although it was only 240 miles from the capital, Vientiane, to the Plain of Jars, it took us seven hours to drive there. It was another 160 miles from the Plain of Jars to Luang Prabang, and it took another seven hours on a road that had a curve every tenth of a mile, going downhill to cross every river and uphill to cross every pass into the next valley. Our driver passed innumerable logging trucks hauling sizable teak logs that had been illegally cut by the government. Half of the cars on those twisty roads had blue license plates.

How far away was China, anyway? One Chinese tourist told us she had driven 2,000 kilometers in two days. I don't know what the roads look like in China, but Laos is not a place for speeding.

The deluge of blue license plates continued in northern Thailand around Chiangmai, where there are four-lane highways with median strips full of bougainvillea. Miles and miles of bougainvillea.

I heard that China will soon be building high-speed trains into Myanmar and Laos. These trains will zip thousands, or hundreds of thousands (dare I say millions?), of Chinese into Southeast Asia. Myanmar has a population of 60 million.

How long do you think it will take for Chinese immigrants to overwhelm Laos with its population of six million? The more populous Myanmar will take longer.

The Chinese are brilliant, really. No military might required. And it only costs one railroad. Just send in the tourists and the immigrants until the Southeast Asian states become virtual vassal states of China.

Jet Drag

IN LATE FEBRUARY I was flying eastward over the Pacific Ocean. Three days later I was wide awake at 2 a.m. as if I were hovering near sunrise over the Atlantic. Apparently my circadian rhythms were coming home via the west with the sunrise, even though my body had headed home by flying east. No wonder I felt slightly separated from my body, as if it had become a foreigner.

On the first flight, from Bangkok to Tokyo, I fell solidly asleep and woke up as the sun rose over India. After the next nap, on the plane from Tokyo to D.C., I woke as the sun rose over Iran. When I finally made it to bed at home, I woke up an hour later, as the sun rose over Turkey. Then I dozed and awoke as the sun rose over England, and there I stayed for three days.

We call it jet lag, but by midday I was dragging so heavily that I could have fallen asleep standing up. Two days after arriving home, I fell asleep for one second while driving on the interstate to my 7:30 p.m. trapeze class. Weariness weakened my strength, my grip on the trapeze bar, and my grip on wakefulness. I was ready to stretch out on the mat under the trapeze and take a nap.

I'm actually okay with waking in the dark hours. I can live perfectly well on five hours of sleep, so I was surprised by the weariness that dragged my eyes closed at 10:00 a.m.,

1:00 p.m., 4:00 p.m., 7:00 p.m., and 8:00 p.m. No amount of napping compensated for the extreme tiredness.

My days and nights were upside down. Oh well, I made hay while the sun wasn't shining, and wrote this blog (cherylwilfong.com) at 2:00 a.m.

CHERYL'S MEMOIRS

Napping on the Davenport

MY DAD WOULD COME home from his office around two or three in the afternoon and take a nap on the davenport. Woe to any child who dared to disturb him. He had this miraculous ability to doze off as soon as his head hit the throw pillow. Nowadays, I can almost do that but it usually takes me about 30 seconds to drift away.

Dad would sleep for about twenty minutes, then put on his overalls, and drove to the horse barn where he worked his harness horses until dark.

My naps are nineteen minutes long. I look at the clock, close my eyes, relax, then open my eyes, look at the clock, and nineteen minutes have passed. I feel *so* much better. Before the nap I felt logy or draggy, and now I'm ready to garden or clean the house.

Really, isn't nineteen minutes about how long a cup of coffee lasts? Why drink coffee in the middle of the afternoon when you could rest your weary bones on the sofa and bounce back into life at full speed? Bill calls it "pushing the reset button." Sleep is so restorative. I'm good for another seven or eight hours.

You could say I learned couch-napping from an early age. That's what sofas are for, right? Before buying any new sofa, just like buying a new-to-me car, I have to see how it naps. Is the sofa long enough? Firm enough? Is the armrest maddeningly high and square? Or low and round?

I have tried cars that don't seem to allow for napping—the seats don't recline, or else you have to laboriously crank the seat down with the twist of an inconveniently-placed knob. Those car designers obviously weren't firing on all four cylinders.

But back to the sofa. After my mother died, I took the throw pillow she had embroidered with turquoise and brown crewel work in the early 1960s. Then, while leafing through an old photo album, I found a picture of myself as a junior in college, taking a nap on the davenport with that very throw pillow under my head. Last year, I finally had to toss out the crewel cover on which so many heads had rested, because the fabric was shredding. I put it in my compost pile, so I expect to see some threads of it in another year or two when I empty out that bin.

Bill introduced me to napping in bed, under a cover or two. This means taking off my pants and socks, but the afternoon cuddle with my sweetie is worth it. According to him, my heavy breathing starts immediately after I've said my last words to him, which could be something like "I don't feel that sleepy right now." *Z-z-z-z.*

Growing up, I would never consider taking a nap in a bed. Well, maybe once in a while, *on* a bed underneath an afghan. My grandmother crocheted and knitted plenty of afghans, so I still have several from which to choose.

After a lunch get-together with friends or at an all-day Saturday workshop, I am completely comfortable lying down on a friend's sofa for a snooze even while everyone else in the room is chatting. If the sofa is full, I pull up a piece of floor and an afghan and let the conversation lull me to the place where words break apart and then become silent.

Oh, wonderful naps! My sister calls it No Activity Planned (NAP). Just the soft sound of deep breathing.

April 10

FIFTY-EIGHT YEARS AGO TODAY I was a flower girl in Aunt Jenny's wedding in Covington, Indiana. She was marrying Keith, now Uncle Keith—a bear of a man who peered out from behind Coke-bottle glasses. Not until after he died in 1999 did I know that he had been in the Battle of the Bulge and then suffered from PTSD for the rest of his life.

On Sunday, April 10, 1955, I just knew that he worked at the Veterans' Administration in Danville, Illinois, and that his parents were The Judge and Bea. Also, Keith read a lot of big, fat books.

I was seven, and my sister Dona was five. My stiff, turquoise organdy dress was size 6X and Dona's was size 6. Aunt Jenny gave us little matching pearl necklaces to wear, and with our white-gloved fingers we dropped rose petals all the way down the aisle of the big brick Methodist church. Well, I had to elbow Dona and whisper to her to remind her to scatter the petals. She was just a little girl and was busy looking around the church.

Aunt Polly, the matron of honor, was also wearing a turquoise dress, but hers was a floor-length formal. Dona and I wore white anklets and patent-leather shoes with a strap across the ankle. We stood beside Aunt Polly and watched her son, three-year-old Stevie, come down the aisle as the ring bearer.

Aunt Jenny wore a white bridal dress. I knew from photos that my mother had worn a suit in her post–World War II wedding in 1946. Aunt Polly had eloped at age 18 in 1950. So those were the three ways you could get married: in a bridal gown, in a suit, or by eloping.

I loved Aunt Jenny, and I was so proud to be her flower girl. I'd already spent two summers with her in Covington—that is, one week each summer. She was so much fun. She taught me how to swim. Also, she was a high school biology teacher.

I visited Aunt Jenny and Uncle Keith for one or two weeks every summer for six years, until I was ten and Aunt Jenny had had her first baby, Leslie, and was pregnant with her second, Kevin.

At age eleven, I went to junior high church camp and in the following years to the high school church camp. Then I began to work during the summers. I seldom saw Aunt Jenny and her family except at Christmas at my grandparents' house and, eventually, at their funerals.

At age 30, in Jungian dream analysis, I realized that although my mother was a good-enough mother, she had been young and not really ready for children. Maybe in a different era she wouldn't have had children until later, and she would have had fewer than four. But she was swept into the post–World War II tide of marriage and babies and the 1950s paternalism of *Father Knows Best*. She stifled her rebellion against my father's strictures—no hugging, for instance—until, at age 29, she had her fourth child.

But I had been well nurtured by Aunt Jenny, who lived next door until I was one. She took me with her everywhere. Then she went to Purdue, and my dad got a job building bleachers for the Purdue football stadium, so I had another six months of being loved to pieces by Aunt Jenny.

After Uncle Keith died, I thought, "Oh, now I can go spend time with Aunt Jenny," but she had cancer of the esophagus and lived less than four months beyond her husband.

I did go for one last visit, for a weekend in December, about two weeks before she died at age 70. I hadn't seen her for nine years, and I was shocked by her frailty. She lived with her oldest daughter, Leslie, and Leslie's husband, as well as her older son, Kevin.

Mostly we chatted and caught up with family news. At any lull in the conversation, my attention was immediately sucked in by the television, which was on 24 hours a day. Then at one point, the three of them—Leslie, Casey, and Kevin—went outdoors for a smoke, leaving me alone with Aunt Jenny. I knew I had just these ten minutes alone with her.

That's when I thanked her for being my aunt, and told her I loved her.

"Oh, Cheryl," she said, "you will never know how much I loved you."

Dear, dear Aunt Jenny.

First Date

THAT FRIDAY NIGHT IN January, we had finished
supper early and the family was just gathering around
the TV to watch *The Red Skelton Show*. Dad didn't abide
nay-sayers, so I'd developed my nonverbal "No way!" I
went to the bathroom and reached for the little bottle of
Suave conditioner. You were supposed to oil your hair with
it before the weekly shampoo on Saturday morning. I always hoped my hair would make me look like a Breck girl,
but it usually just lay flat on my head and waved in various
directions. My pageboy always had a flip section, and my
flip always had a pageboy curl.

I was just combing the Suave into my hair, so I could
sleep on it, when the phone rang. I looked into the mirror.
Boy. My hair was really oily now.

"Cheryl. The phone's for you."

I walked out the bathroom, across the living room to
the big black receiver lying a short distance from the rotary
dial with a circle of paper in the center. EVergreen 8-2856.

"Hello."

"Hi Cheryl. This is Joe."

"Joe?" I'd never received a phone call from a boy in my
entire sixteen-year-old life.

"Yeah. I wondered whether you'd like to go see Peter
Nero at Anderson College tonight."

CHERYL WILFONG

67

"Just a minute. Let me ask." I put my hand over the end of the receiver you talked into. "Dad. It's Joe Wisehart. He wants to know if I can go to hear Peter Nero at Anderson College tonight."

Dad had a strict rule: No dates for my sister or me until we were sixteen. So far, it hadn't been an issue for me. I had just turned sixteen a month earlier.

My younger sister, Dona, was the one who always had a steady boyfriend. And she couldn't ride in a car alone with him, not even his father's brand-new powder-blue Thunderbird.

"Sure," said Dad.

I was shocked but I repeated into the phone, "Sure."

"Okay. I'll pick you up in twenty minutes."

"Okay." I hung up.

"He's picking me up in twenty minutes." I looked at Mother. "What am I going to do with my hair?" I pulled my fingers through my stringy, oily shoulder-length hair.

"Do a French roll," Mom said from the corner of the sofa, where she was ensconced with her feet tucked up beside her as she leafed through a *Family Circle* magazine.

I headed to the bathroom and slicked my hair back into a French roll. I'd done it often enough that I had mastered the art of holding it with my left hand while prying bobby pins open with my teeth and right thumb and index finger.

I zoomed into the bedroom I shared with my sister, went to the closet, picked a gray-and-white houndstooth wool suit with a Chanel jacket that I had sewn myself. Slip, girdle, hose, heels, white blouse with a Peter Pan collar. I hurriedly shifted everything in my purse into a gray pocketbook that matched my gray heels.

EVERY GOOD THING

I heard a knock on the front door, and then my mother's voice. "Come in, Joe."

I knew from Dad's tirades that we were never to keep anyone waiting. So I walked out of my room straight to the coat closet. "Hi Joe." I barely noticed him as I got out my coat and he helped me on with it.

"Have a good time," said Dad.

I led Joe out the front door. He opened the passenger door of his red-and-white 1961 Chevy Impala.

Joe and I talked every day in Advanced Algebra, Wilfong sitting just in front of Wisehart, and in the three minutes between classes we'd chatter away. And we chatted that evening as well. It was the first piano concert I'd ever been to, and I felt very sophisticated, in my suit, with a date, listening to the popular pianist, Peter Nero. Joe and I talked all the way back to my house, where he held the car door open for me and walked me to my front door. "Thanks, Joe," I said. "See you Monday."

After my date with Joe, I didn't speak to him for the rest of the year. I avoided him in the halls, at the lockers. I was too . . . well, what? Shy, yes. Self-conscious, yes. Embarrassed, definitely. But also too afraid of opening the Pandora's box that Dad had repeatedly lectured my sister and me against. I didn't want to know. I didn't want to feel the stirrings of whatever it might have been.

And also, at some deeper level, I didn't want to stay in Hancock County, Indiana. I wanted out.

At the 40th reunion of the Eastern Hancock class of 1965, half of our graduating class of 82 showed up. After dinner, the organizer handed the microphone to each classmate in turn and we recited the nutshell version of our lives.

How many of those women said, "I got married in June (or July or October) after we graduated"? How many of the ones who went to college married their high school sweethearts? Four of the six couples from our class are still married to each other.

That evening of our reunion I had a good time talking to the woman who had managed the high school cafeteria for fifteen years, and my junior high friend who remembers the class motto and has always tried to live up to it. "In Ourselves Our Future Lies." I chatted with my former neighbor, Roger Wallace, who's still farming and who complained about high taxes. One classmate is the president of Greenfield Banking Company, and he approves Roger's farm loan on a year-to-year basis.

Several male classmates had retired after working for 35 years at a General Motors subsidiary.

"Oh, were you NAFTAed?" I asked Louis Calvert, who had gone through all twelve grades with me.

"Yes," he said. "When I went down to Mexico to do consulting, the factory was on NAFTA Street. Of course, that consulting job only lasted a few months."

The drum majorette who had been my best friend in elementary school married the boy whose 1963 class ring she wove with angora yarn every morning on the school bus. Now he owns the John Deere dealership in town.

I saw Joe Wisehart for the first time in 40 years. "Oh, Joe," I said. "Please forgive me."

"Forgive you?" he smiled as he put his arm around my shoulder. "Forgive you for what?"

I could feel the light pressure of his arm on the long hair that cascades down my back. "You were the only boy who asked me out on a date in high school. And after we went to see Peter Nero, I never spoke to you again."

"I don't remember that," he said. "But I do remember Peter Nero."

We chatted on. He lived outside of Chicago, in Oak Park, Illinois, and worked as a real estate broker.

"The Shirley Historical Society has a copy of your book about the Nez Perce Trail," he said.

I looked at him, puzzled.

"I gave them my copy, along with my letter jacket." Joe is a history buff, like me.

"After my dad bought your dad's arrowhead collection," I said, "he donated it to Ball State."

Soon we were discussing his second marriage (no children from his first), and from there we went to spiritual paths.

"Remember I was brought up fundamentalist Nazarene?" he said. "Well, I've been going to the Unitarian church for 30 years, but I'm about to convert to Catholicism. My second wife's a Catholic. What about you?"

I told him of my Buddhist path in less than five minutes, and then because he was there without his wife, and I was there without Bill, Joe sat down beside me for dinner.

I felt instantly at home with Joe, something I've only felt a very few times in my life, and I knew that if I'd opened up to him at age sixteen, my life would have been completely different.

My VISTA Boyfriend

A T AGE 22, I was happy, very happy, during my year as a VISTA volunteer—it remains one of the peak experiences of my life.[6] Eight of us recent college graduates were assigned to four projects scattered across a couple hundred miles in southwestern Utah. We spent every weekend together, often driving to a nearby national park such as Zion or Bryce.

As much as I loved my year as a VISTA volunteer, I wasn't ready to re-up. I had fallen in love with Rod, one of my co-workers, who was from Hawai'i. I felt proud to hold the hand of this handsome six-foot-tall Japanese-American as we walked down the street in Cedar City.

Southern Utah was a bastion of Mormonism; the area south of Cedar City was called Dixie. We VISTAs worked with Native Americans—Southern Paiutes mostly, but also a few Navajo migrants—whom the Mormons referred to as Lamanites, meaning those with brown skin. If the Indians would just pray hard enough, they too could become

---

6.   VISTA—Volunteers In Service To America--was founded in 1965. It was incorporated into AmeriCorps in 1993.

"white and delightsome" like the mostly-blond Mormons who surrounded us.[7]

At the end of our year of service, Utah didn't feel like home and my seven VISTA buddies were returning to their own home bases. Rod had signed up for another year of VISTA in his home state of Hawai'i. I was still intent on seeing the world, and so, at the end of our year, I wrote to my 41-year-old bachelor Uncle Harold and asked if I could come live with him in Waikiki. He wrote back, "Yes." So I accompanied Rod as he headed west.

My parents arrived in Honolulu two weeks later to visit Harold, Dad's youngest brother, and me.

This was my attempt at world peace: greeting my parents with leis as they stepped off the airplane. Dad looked at my boyfriend and saw the young Japs he had killed 25 years earlier. I gave Mom and Dad a hug, and Rod and I hung around their necks the fragrant frangipani flowers that we had strung together. My dad wearing flowers. Well, anything was possible, after all.

I had reserved a little Toyota rental car for my dad, knowing full well he only bought American cars and that he would never in his life buy a Japanese product. But here in Hawai'i, where everything had to be imported and everything was expensive, small cars that used less gas made so much more sense. He named that little white Toyota "Tojo."[8] I only vaguely understood the implications.

---

7.   "White and delightsome" appears in *The Book of Mormon*, 2 Nephi 30:6.
8.   Tojo was the prime minister of Japan who was responsible for World War II in the Pacific theater. In the United States, his name had the same flavor as "Hitler."

Another thing I was not attuned to was how brusquely my father talked to Rod's parents when they met. I was not aware of the fine emotional tuning and politeness inherent in the Japanese-American culture. To me, Dad was just being Dad, and I didn't give his gruffness a second thought.

Although I didn't know it until after he was dead, Dad delivered a clear message to his Waikiki brother: "Get her away from the Jap."

I could imagine golden children of the future as race lines blurred, but my Hawaiian boyfriend was more at home with his family, who also believed in racial purity. Rod had grown up in the pineapple fields, and he knew all the derogatory words for any number of mixed-race combinations: Japanese-Chinese, -Filipino, -Hawaiian, -*haole*.

Our fate was sealed, though it took a few months for it to work itself out. Rod did not want a *haole* wife and mixed-race children. He wanted a woman who would cater to his needs. I could not understand his drive to earn a lot of money by going to medical school and becoming a doctor. So we parted, peacefully, but still with some unspent longing. Our passion pulled apart by skin color.

John's Birthday

IN LATE MAY, I told Bill that I had messaged an old boyfriend on the occasion of his seventieth birthday. It was one of those things I didn't need to tell him, yet I felt secretive not telling him. I could feel the rationalizations about why it wasn't important, but that line of thinking just confirmed to me that I was hiding something, if not from Bill, then from myself.

I've adhered to a strict policy of not friending old boyfriends on Facebook. I don't even look. But John, with his Polish last name, was easy to find.

Funny how such intimate boyfriends utterly drop off the list of friends. There was love, if not the lasting kind, at least a temporary sort of love, a touching of the hearts. When we release that temporary connection, we think the love has gone, and yet affection has only gone underground, to become poignant, many years later, when we hear of the other person's death.

In my late twenties, John was a way for me to avoid loneliness. I never, ever had a single thought of marriage. And so I whittled away four and a half years. He was a lover of women and conversation, so I didn't think too closely about what he was doing when he moved up to central Vermont and I visited him one weekend every three or four weeks.

I stopped all correspondence when he got married at age 44, ten years after we had stopped dating. After a 24-year hiatus, I saw John two years ago at the memorial service for Norman, who had hired me as the bookkeeper for the Putney Food Coop when he and John were co-managing it in 1974. In an instant, I was swept up by John's charisma, and I was happy to have Bill standing by my side. My comparing mind settled happily on Bill even as I felt a warm heart tug toward John.

What's the point of remembering birthdays, anyway? Is it really an altruistic act of recalling the specialness of that person? Or is the ego hiding in there, "Heh, heh, heh. I remembered your birthday. Aren't I good? Aren't I better than those who forgot?"

What *is* the point of remembering a birthday?

I've always thought of birthdays as personal holidays celebrated by just a few close friends or family members, but now Facebook has made the birthday list overwhelming. When I look at my iPad calendar, all I see are birthdays, three or five every single day. My personal schedule of what I am doing when is eclipsed by hundreds of birthdays. Ai-yi-yi. Too much information I don't want to know.

I happen to have a mind that remembers birthdays, phone numbers, and zip codes. Many friends ask, "How do you do that?" They seem to feel diminished because they don't remember my birthday, but days and months go by and their minds are uncluttered by birthdayism. Perhaps they are the actual winners.

So, happy seventieth birthday, John. My god, how did we get this old? I haven't seen your wife in 25 years, and I've never met your grown-up children. I still have a few mementos around the house—two of your watercolors and a brass-and-glass bowl that you made at the Penland School of Crafts in North Carolina. Should I send them back to you now? Or wait till your eightieth birthday? Or your death?

Because more than you, I am remembering myself as I was. When I met you, I had just discovered that my best friend was dating a guy I was in love with, and then a year later, they married. Many years later, Bill would reflect to me, "Oh, my dear Cheryl, that was no contest. She was and still is foxy."

When I was 26, I couldn't see that big picture. I was still feeling the sting from my loss, and there was big bear John, and he was lonely, too. So I spent my late twenties in that loose relationship, which closed off other possibilities for me, but not for him.

It's a lukewarm era to remember, and why would I want to anyway? Other than the temporary love that gave me some solace and stability as I continued my climb out of the depression that was my twenty-fifth year.

Nonnie

WHEN I WAS 37, I called my grandmother one Saturday morning. "Hi Nonnie," I said. "I'm thinking about having a child, and I wanted your opinion."

My biological clock was ticking, and my very best friend, Mary Beth, who had three children, kept telling me all about the joys of motherhood—single motherdom for her. She thought it was an experience I shouldn't miss.

I'd been fatalistic toward the subject of children, figuring that if I met a man before I turned 42, then we'd have children. Men. Not my best subject. I'd been in love only twice in my life. Once at age 22, and once again at age 35. Okay. I was *still* in love with Harlan, but he'd broken up with me because, oh, I don't know. Because I was too much like him, because I suspected him of being an alcoholic (which he vehemently denied), because I was too wishy-washy about having children.

I'd even taken a six-week class on how to decide whether to have children. Harlan didn't come with me, and I wondered about that at the time. Later I figured out, he'd already decided—Children: yes. Me: no. Toward the end of that relationship, I took more risks, failed to use my diaphragm. But unlike age 25, when I got pregnant twice in one year from having sex an equal number of times, with two different IUDs, nothing came of taking the risk. As a might-have-been mother, I lost my opportunity. No man on the horizon, my clock ticking. Was I going to regret this path of a single life that I seemed unable to veer off of? Should I have a child? I thought I should ask my 82-year-old grandmother.

"Why would you want to ruin your life like that?" she said. "You've got a nice life."

Nonnie thought I traveled a lot and saw the world. I was on my fourth career: cross-cultural trainer, human services administrator, magazine editor, and now accountant. I sure hoped this career wouldn't last too long. Trying to be a yuppie in the city was b-o-r-i-n-g.

I knew intuitively what my grandmother was saying. We were talking across an extremely wide generation gap. She was from the era when an illegitimate child ruined a girl's reputation in a small town forever. I was from the sexual revolution, where everything was possible.

But beyond that chasm, I saw my white-haired grandmother, sitting alone day after day in her recliner by the picture window, her three daughters and ten grandchildren and twenty great-grandchildren nowhere in sight. Fast-forward mothering a baby a few decades, and there you are: alone. A sharper aloneness for the love you bear all those dear ones who sprang from your loins.

They drop in once a week or once a year, and then rush off after an hour or two, so busy with their own lives. And there you are with the TV and the ticking clock, knitting love and prayers into slippers for each and every one of them.

Nonnie died two and half years after that conversation. I stopped hearing the false alarm of my bio-illogical clock, moved back to my house in the Vermont woods, and worked one more year as an accountant.

Nonnie. When I was seven, eight, nine years old, I'd spend a week with her each summer. We'd play cards and then we'd write stories. Sometimes together, sometimes separately. We'd each fill a page with make-believe and then read to each other. Oh, how she would laugh at the silly stories we concocted.

Twenty years later she would say to me, "You should write a book about your travels." I didn't travel *that* much, I thought. I just wrote lots of letters from far-away places: three months in Europe, living in Florida with my first boy-friend (I didn't tell her that part), being a VISTA volunteer in Utah, following my first true love to Hawai'i, doing an internship for my master's degree in Guatemala, driving around the West for three months. I'd retire from one career and go traveling before I started another. What's to write about that?

Then one day, when I was 39, my dad said to me for perhaps the tenth time in my life, "You should write a book." Since Dad and Nonnie agreed on practically nothing else in life, I finally received the message. I finally took his advice. And then, while I was on the road again, doing the research for my book on the Nez Perce Trail, Nonnie died.

What happens after death? I guess I go with the school of thought that believes that souls look at their recent lives and learn from their mistakes and study something or other, I'm not sure what. Perhaps they look and see their loved ones struggling on through life without them. And then they look again and several months have passed, and life has gone on.

Right after Nonnie died, I prayed to her to help me meet a man. I believe that right after a person dies, they're still pretty interested in those they've left behind. So praying to them has a big, if sometimes slow, effect.

Eleven months later, I met Bill. An unlikely match for me, but there he was, a 52-year-old Tigger, and there I was, a 40-year-old Jane-of-all-trades.

Three months after that, Bill introduced me to his mother, who was just the age Nonnie was when she died. I bonded with Mabel immediately, despite the silver spoon in her Social Register mouth. Mabel knew and sounded just like Katharine Hepburn. Mabel was too old to garden anymore, but when she saw my greenhouse, she told me how she'd had a greenhouse built at every house she'd ever lived in.

A few months later, I met Bill's oldest daughter—a college graduate who was fledging in Puerto Rico as a journalist. She was her poet-mother's only child and had no need of a stepmother, not after she'd been consigned to the Cinderella role by Bill's second wife. So Jeni and I became friends simply because we both loved and were exasperated by the same person—Bill.

Another two years of messy divorce passed before I met Bill's younger daughter. Right after Lauren's fourteenth birthday, she'd checked herself into the Brattleboro Retreat and I brought her daffodils, which turned out to be a good choice because Lauren liked to garden.

The big advantage of Lauren's week in a psychiatric hospital was that it broke the stalemate of her mother not following through on complying with court-ordered visitation rights for Bill. The divorce finally over, I painted our guest room pale pink, thinking of Lauren's future overnights with us.

She only came a few times before she went to a boarding school for special children. And then she got weirder and weirder, moaning for days until they sent her home to her mother.

She completed her freshman year, although she really didn't do the required schoolwork. Then one summer night, her mother took her for an evaluation at the Dartmouth-Hitchcock psychiatric ward. From there, a state police car took her in handcuffs to the children's unit at the New Hampshire State Hospital, where she spent the remainder of her high school years.

After a while, Lauren would occasionally come spend the night with us on a weekend. She claimed it was the Haldol that made her so restless that she roamed the house all night and left the lights on, the refrigerator door open, and a mess on the kitchen counters. In my fury, I tried to scream her into normality, and I even hurled a bottle of mouthwash down the basement stairs. To no avail. Lauren started fondly calling me Cher-yell, and I grieved the loss of my last chance at stepmothering. When, a year later, in 1994, we heard the diagnosis of Asperger's syndrome, I breathed a sigh of relief because it made *so* much sense.

My fantasies of stepmothering died a tearful death as Lauren graduated from the New Hampshire State Hospital to a halfway house, where she drove the other residents crazy with constant moaning and obsessive-compulsive behavior. When Mabel died, I prayed hard to her about helping Lauren.

She moved into a duplex in Concord owned by her

mother, who then evicted her and dumped her in Brattle-boro, close to Bill, while she moved with her new husband to New Mexico. My neighbor reported seeing Lauren talking to parking meters on Main Street. Evicted again, she moved to an apartment in Putney, then to a locked unit in a psychiatric hospital, then to another halfway house, and then, just as she was about to be put into the locked unit again, she fled. A month later, a shopkeeper in Key West called Bill to ask if she was a runaway. A few months later, the hospital at Mount Shasta called because she had frostbite. They put her on a bus headed out of town. Sometimes Bill wouldn't hear from her for a month or two. To make a very l-o-n-g story short, Lauren finally settled in New Mexico near her mother a year and a half later.

Meanwhile, Jeni had returned from six years in Puerto Rico, met a man named Jim, worked for the *Boston Globe*, and gotten married. They had moved to her new job at the *Orange County Register* in southern California. In their mid-30s, in the year 2000, Jeni and Jim had a baby and named her Chloe.

Jim's mother and dad had seven children who all, except for Jim, lived nearby. Chloe is their seventeenth grandchild. Jeni's mother calls her every morning, and Chloe's middle name is hers: Elizabeth. So this little girl has the full complement of grandparents, and I wondered about my own fifth-wheel role.

But Jeni said Chloe was really lucky to have three grandmothers and wanted to know Bill's and my grandparent names. I chose to be called Nonnie. And that's when the miracle occurred: even though I have no children, I have grandchildren.

DAD

No Regrets

WHEN I WAS 45, I made the commitment to myself to visit my 75-year-old father one weekend every three months. This meant leaving Bill home alone and taking a half day off work on Friday (usually I could use comp time), driving to the airport, and flying to Indianapolis via some hub such as Cleveland, Philadelphia, or Washington. Six hours after leaving work, I walked off my plane with my shoulder bag, down the Jetway, and through the door to the concourse.

There I would see Dad, waiting for me—bald with a fringe of white hair around the edge of his head, Varilux glasses in the aviator style. He had once been five-foot-ten, but was now an inch or so shorter, about 30 pounds overweight, solid from working his horses every day. He had his farmer tan, even in January.

Imagine him now in a light blue shirt and tan chinos, probably wearing either a feed cap or a jacket that says "Trotter Range"—the name of his horse farm. "Hi, Sis," he says gruffly, and we give each other a side-to-side hug. We walk wordlessly down the concourse of Weir Cook Airport.

H. Weir Cook was an ace in World War I and a cousin of Dad's mother. He died in a plane crash in New Caledonia during World War II while Dad was fighting in the Solomon Islands. But all that is history—never talked about.

We walk out the doors of the airport and across the roadway to his Lincoln Continental parked at a parking meter.

"Did you wait long?" I ask.

"Nope," he says. "just got here ten minutes ago." He's trained me to be on time, which means arriving a little early.

I put my bag in the trunk and push the lid closed.

"You don't have to slam it," he says testily. "It closes by itself." I watch as the trunk lid whirs down the last two inches to its fully closed position.

He drives. Always. I sit in the passenger seat. No sooner are we on I-465 than I feel the first sneeze coming on. I'm allergic to his car and all the invisible horse dander. I see he has a small box of Kleenex sitting on the hump of the floor between us. He never used to carry Kleenex, so this mind-over-matter man must have the occasional nasal tickle himself.

I try to be my fully adult self instead of automatically slipping into my silent-teenager-at-home-with-my-parents self. "How are the horses?" I ask. I don't give a damn about his horses, but this is one of his favorite topics of conversation. He's spent the past 40 years trying to build what he calls the horse industry of Indiana.

Those are just words to me. Yes, I know he had a horse named Superstar Ranger, good enough to race in the Hambletonian. Yes, I know the Indiana Trotting and Pacing Horse Association gave him an award for having the best two-year-old trotter in Indiana. Yawn. Not until after he dies in 1997, just before his eightieth birthday, will I understand the import of that aspect of his life's work.

Yeah, yeah, yeah, I think to myself. But I try to keep conversation going on the 30-minute drive to his home in Carmel, on the north side of Indianapolis.

I choose to visit my dad one weekend every three months because, really, how much longer will he live? He and my divorced mother are not going to live forever. I tell myself I don't want to have any regrets, even though I am unable to articulate what regrets I might possibly have.

I stay at Dad's house in order to see him in the evenings and in the morning at 6:30 before he goes out for coffee at McDonald's with his cronies. In the evenings, I sit in the living room with him and watch *Jeopardy* and The History Channel. TV is not my idea of quality time, but I have to assume there's a certain joining, a certain togetherness in just being company to my mostly silent father.

Mother is more fun, her refrigerator is more interesting, and I'd rather stay with her, but she's an alcoholic, and I just can't take the slurring, the irrational monologues, the soap operas, the too-late nights, and the silent mornings.

Until she picks me up at eleven, I walk across the paddock to my brother Beau's house. He has four children, ages seven to twelve, and I play with them and visit with my brother and sister-in-law.

While Dad is working his horses, Mom and I go shopping and out to lunch and to a movie. I drive her car because she's subject to panic attacks and various shards of anxiety. The heavily traveled streets make her nervous, so she directs me along side streets.

On Sunday mornings, I go with Dad on his weekly visit to his remaining relatives. His oldest sister, Anna, in her late eighties, has macular degeneration. His youngest living sister, Ruth, in her mid-seventies, had a leg amputated due to diabetes, just like their mother. His sister-in-law Dorothy—a month younger than Ruth—is the widow of his favorite brother. He doesn't stay long, maybe fifteen minutes at each one. As soon as the conversation sags, he gets up and leaves.

Then we drive by familiar places and stop at the house Dad built in 1949, the house where we grew up, and where my brother Paul now lives. Paul's wife, Debbie, is a handicrafter and so the rustic-log-cabin chic decor is totally different from what I grew up with. They've added a family room, a three-car garage, and a wood-working shop for Debbie, and they've dug a pond in what used to be the woods behind the house, but I still recognize a basic homeness as I am flooded with memories by every room in the house and every tree in the yard.

It's on these 40-minute drives to Greenfield, and then back again to Carmel, that I'm most likely to catch what I came for this weekend from this inarticulate man: a single sentence. Four sentences per year. Like: "I wish I'd spent more time with you when you were kids." That's as close to asking forgiveness as he can come, and that's enough for me.

My father died just before my fiftieth birthday, and I have no regrets at all about those five years of four inconvenient, and often boring, weekend trips to Indiana each year.

Dad's Heart

MY FATHER'S DEATH CERTIFICATE says that he died of congestive heart failure. That surprised me, because I had thought he died of kidney failure. His uric acid levels started climbing when he was 74. At 75 he had a port implanted in his belly, and when that healed, he started home dialysis—"exchanges." Four times a day, he drained a liter of fluid out of his abdomen and then dripped a liter of saline solution in. This went on for four years until he got an infection, which scarred the peritoneum and made the exchanges less effective. You could say that he was slowly poisoned by his own uric acid. He just couldn't excrete the toxins.

Although he made the best of it, the toxins of his life built up. Two people he loved died when he was still in school—first, his grandfather Pappy, then grandmother Mammy. In 1930 his twelve-year-old friend Myron was killed on a bicycle while he, Ralph—my future father—was perched on the handlebars. In 1931 his next older brother, Roscoe, died. And when he was a junior in high school, his father died from injuries after a truck accident.

Ralph was a rascal, and at times even a prankster, but still he took on the responsibility for his widowed mother and four younger siblings. He worked but couldn't keep a job in the last years of the Great Depression, when labor was so easy to find and an employer could save himself a daily wage or two by firing people before payday.

At age 24, in 1942, Ralph was drafted into the Army and sent to the South Pacific with the Tropical Lightning Division. The only story I heard, because he never talked about the war, was that he once jumped into a foxhole and there was a Jap. Obviously, the Jap did not survive, but Ralph, the farm boy who had butchered cows and pigs and wrung the necks of chickens, did. His sisters said he came back from the war "different."

One of the good things that was different about him was that rising in the ranks, from private to corporal to sergeant, had given him confidence to be the boss. By using his rascal ways, he had gotten things done. His squad was the only one that had electricity in their tents at night, because Ralph had repaired a Japanese generator. Since he and his buddies were the mechanics for the Jeeps, tanks, half-tracks, etc., they made sure the generator traveled by Jeep to the next bivouac.

Ralph always had a lightning temper. Nowadays, we would call him a "rage-aholic," but back then it was normal. And a minute later, the air was clear, and he was smiling, and he loved you—wife, child, employee. Forget the roar, the slap, the spanking, the shout. It was over. The toxins had been released.

But the deeper hurts lasted longer—his drunk wife, his alcoholic brother, his drinking son who couldn't afford his divorces. These were the long, slow toxins that acidified Ralph's heart.

Congestive heart failure is the heart working harder and less efficiently, so that the heart becomes too large.

Ralph loved us all—his four children who didn't live up to his hopes and who lived lives he couldn't understand; his wife of 37 years, even after the eventual divorce; his married girlfriend; his eight adult brothers and sisters, all with their individual failings and spats; his nieces and nephews whom he employed for a summer or a year; the bookkeeper who, for 30 years, stood up to him almost every day and argued about money or his next great idea, and thereby made him successful; the 50 employees to whom he gave Christmas turkeys and loans when they needed them. He loved his dozens of standard-bred horses and all the horse people who couldn't scrape a living together with their racehorses.

His heart encompassed all of us with a deep generosity, seasoned heavily with his own opinions and a flash of lightning, until his heart was just too big and couldn't support him any longer.

The Office

THE OFFICE WAS A member of our family for as long as I can remember. The first of Dad's offices that I recall from the mid-1950s was a house on East 38th Street in Indianapolis. The room next-door to Dad's two-room office was occupied by Oscar Josie—a short, well-tanned man with thin white hair and a trim white mustache. Old Man Josie—as Dad always called him—encouraged Dad to get into land development. He also gave Dad two harness horses, which Dad later said were worth as much as he had paid for them. Dad bought one more horse and that was the beginning of Trotter Range. Those two pivotal decisions—horses and land development—ruled the remaining 45 years of Dad's life.

In 1954 he developed his first subdivision, named Lady Hamilton Estates and located on 111th Street in Carmel, Indiana. Its one oval street was named Cheryl Lane.[9] Bob and Esther Yohler lived across the street from Lady Hamilton, and somehow Dad became good friends with them. Bob Yohler had an orchid greenhouse, so for the next several years Mom and Dona and I each received an orchid corsage to wear to church on Easter Sunday.

---

9. Sometime later the short connector to 111th Street was renamed Chevy Lane and the oval became Beechwood Drive.

EVERY GOOD THING

In 1961 The Office moved to an old four-room house that smelled permanently of damp basement. It had a cistern with nine-inch-long carp swimming lazily in it. This office was located on 82nd Street, east of Castleton and right across from Dad's development, Sleepy Hollow, which had 25 lots.[10]

Edith, the middle-aged blonde secretary who had lost both her index fingers under a lawn mower (in two separate accidents) sat in the front room. Bob Yohler, who had retired from orchids, had a desk in the back room, and Dad's office was in the side room.

When we kids visited The Office on occasional Sunday afternoons in the spring and fall, while Dad was sitting in his car, trying, in vain, to sell lots to young couples with young children, we made a beeline for the 1920s kitchen that had a little old refrigerator filled with pale-green-glass bottles of Coca-Cola (6.5 ounces), green bottles of 7 Up(seven ounces), and clear bottles of Fanta (orange and grape). There were only a few bottles of TaB, a diet cola, which had only recently come onto the market. We'd entertain each other by guessing where the others' Coke bottles had come from—the city of the processing plant was stamped on the bottom of the glass bottle. Whose Coke came from farthest away?

The summer after my freshman year in college, I went to work for Dad there. The depressed secretary stopped coming to work four days after I began, so on Friday I went

10. Sleepy Hollow, just a mile east of the little town of Castleton, was ahead of its time. Two years after Dad left Castleton, I-465 was completed, and the town boomed into multiple malls, shopping centers, and plazas, along with square mile after square mile of housing developments.

ahead and wrote out the paychecks, writing the date carefully on each one—6/6/66. Fortunately, Edith had taught me how to use the FICA chart with the federal withholding tax chart on the other side, and the Indiana withholding tax chart, so I could calculate the next week's payroll for the eight employees. I felt very adult, being Dad's secretary. I also drank as much TaB as I wanted.

Dad interviewed possible secretaries a couple of weeks later. I liked the careful-seeming 40-something woman, but Dad hired the blonde bombshell who had three young children and needed a nine-to-three job. Her name was Sue House.

Things had changed a lot by the summer of 1967. Dad had bought (i.e., borrowed the money to buy) a square mile of farmland in Clay Township, population 3,000, just south of Carmel. The development was named Woodland Springs, and ten selected custom builders constructed dozens, and eventually hundreds, of homes for executives and their families.

Both Dona and I went to work at The Office, which was now in a little old farmhouse on 116th Street in Carmel, one block east of Keystone. This five-room house had three full-time employees, in addition to Dad. Sitting in the front room with Sue was a new bookkeeper in her late thirties named Pat. Dad sat in the back office. Ken Thompson, a commercial real estate broker, sat in the middle office, followed later by Tom Barnes. Finally, after all those lean years, Dad was doing a land-office business—literally.

Under Pat's watchful eye, Dona and I mastered the art of the ten-key adding machine and added long columns of numbers without looking at the keypad. We learned to

EVERY GOOD THING

post checks in a journal and to balance the monthly bank statements. We worked in that The Office for three summers, filing the bills that came in every day, paying them on the tenth of the month, running the checks through the Burroughs check protector machine, then filing the bills in each vendor's folder. We typed letters with their carbon copies, and we typed up property deeds. We calculated equipment-rental rates for each of the four different kinds of bulldozers, backhoes, earth movers, excavators, and various tractors and sent the road- and sewer-construction bills to other land developers. We calculated weekly payroll for twenty-two people and typed up the quarterly payroll tax reports. We barely had time to go to the kitchen for a soda, but Sue House spent most of her time in there hanging out with J.R., the construction foreman.

Much later Dona would say, "We went to the Pat Emmert School of Bookkeeping." For the rest of our lives, we could look at any small organization or our friends' projects in dollars and cents, ask key questions, and guesstimate profit and loss on the back of an envelope. And, of course, we always balanced our own checkbooks, every month.

Then, in 1970, I graduated from college and Dona got married. When I came back in 1971 for a visit, The Office had moved into a trailer on the northwest corner of 116th and Keystone, where Keystone Shopping Center was being built. Pat and Sue complained about how cold they were in this The Office during the winter. Our cousin Susan, who was Beau's age, worked in The Office during the summer of 1973.

Sue House left and was replaced by Marilyn when, in 1974, Dad left Carmel, now with a booming population of

30,000, and moved into another The Office just off 146th Street and U.S. 31 in Westfield. He had purchased four farms on 1,340 acres—two square miles of farmland—the Two Gaits Farm, the Happy T Farm, the Berman Farm, and the Senator Farm. The latter had been owned by the trainer and driver of Greyhound, the fastest trotter in the 1930s; his record of 1:55¼ stood for 30 years. He was called The Horse of the Century.

This two-story brick house had been a grand home in the 1930s. The front staircase curved up from the spacious foyer. Three of the four bedrooms-cum-offices upstairs had their own full bathrooms. Downstairs, the former living room held Marilyn's desk, Pat's desk, and had room for one more woman. Dad's desk was in the former dining room, and he looked out a big picture window. The kitchen was quite usable and sunny, and a modern refrigerator held not only soda, but also various juices. I gravitated to the tomato juice since I no longer drank sodas.

Beau had worked for Dad mowing hay every summer since he was eleven, but after his sophomore year in college, he too attended the Pat Emmert School of Bookkeeping at The Office for two summers, in 1975 and 1977.

As Dad became successful and gave birth to one brainchild company after another, the staff expanded until women (called "the girls") were crammed into every nook and cranny of The Office, while each man had his own individual office—Jeff Henson, the accountant, Harold Egger, the commercial real estate broker, and eventually, in 1986, Beau, who returned from his ministerial training and gave up his UPS day job to become general manager.

This The Office was a place where I felt at home,

especially when we four children-of-Ralph held annual meetings, starting in 1985. We were all in our thirties. Dad was 67 years old, with absolutely no thought of an estate plan. So we began our meetings with an inventory of his holdings and his indebtedness. Personally, I was terrified that if he dropped dead, I/we would be responsible for a few million dollars of debt. Interest rates had reached their zenith of 20 percent in 1980 and bounced around at 17 and 18 percent during the early 1980s.

For a few years, Dona and I did special projects during our annual week in The Office: one year we researched 401(k) plans, one year we wrote a manual of personnel policies, and another year we did a system analysis of computerizing the bookkeeping.

For twenty years Pat had done the books by hand—now more than ten sets of books for all the various companies and partnerships—just as she'd done books for the twenty years before she came to work in The Office. She was not about to change to this newfangled push-a-button computer thing.

In 1987 Pat was moved upstairs to her own office, with one other, usually empty, desk. She felt this being kicked upstairs was a demotion, rather like an old mare being turned out to pasture. Then she realized how quiet it was, away from Ralph and the hubbub of people coming and going.

My sister and brothers and I continued our annual meetings. While I was getting a master's degree in psychology in the early 1990s, I did financial consulting for my brother Beau and sorted out the mishmash of money being loaned from one company to another depending on who needed what when. I broke Dad's company, Fine Builders, into four divisions: construction, land and rental properties (including a shopping center), the water utility, and the horses. Finally, each "division" could be judged on its own merit. If the construction company didn't break even in January and February, the muddy months, it would show a loss at the end of the year. The horses always lost money; now it was clear that Dad's hobby was costing him $100,000 to $200,000 a year. The land and rental properties were the cash cows. And the water and sewer utility was so complicated and bound by regulations that costs would always be dragging down the income.

My weeklong consulting visits every two months gave me a good income of $50 an hour, and I came to have a good feel for Dad's estate. Sometimes Dad just suffered me in silence; sometimes he thought I wanted my inheritance. He rained his lightning bolts on me once or twice a week, and Beau nicknamed me The Lightning Rod. But my brother, armed with budgets and cash flow projections, was now able to fly through the money storms and actually put an estate plan in place.

In 1997 the land that The Office sat on was sold for a shopping plaza, so The Office was jacked up and put on a truck. It took two long June days to move it four blocks, and another day to drive it onto its new foundation. During the process, the staff moved out and crammed themselves into rented quarters for six months while Dad's desk moved to the office in a barn at the Westwind Farm.

Was it just coincidence that shortly after The Office left its moorings, 79-year-old Ralph lost his? He stood up suddenly at home and fainted. He woke up to find he had broken his right ankle. For a few weeks he motored around his house on a little scooter, and (don't tell his children) he drove his Lincoln Continental with his left foot on the gas pedal. That summer he looked older and more peaked. In August, he got an infection in his peritoneum; in October, he had to be hospitalized for three days. On October 31, my sister and I arrived to join our brothers for Dad's final days.

The staff moved back into The Office on October 29. Dad dragged himself in to look at the new siting and died on November 5.

Keystone Square Shopping Center was sold the following week, so four employees went to the new owner. Two months later, all the horses were sold, and Trotter Range was disbanded. Three more employees left.

As executor, Beau maintained the status quo for four years. Then, in early 2002, he sold Hamilton-Western Utilities, a water and sewer company. Eleven more employees went to the new owners, seven to the Town of Westfield, and four to the Town of Carmel. Since Wilfong Construction had had the monopoly on installing water and sewer lines, the sale of the utility put them out of business. Its 24 employees had to look for new jobs. The mini-empire of Ralph Wilfong became weaker and weaker until just the skeleton staff of Beau and Pat was rattling around in the thirteen-room office with five bathrooms.

Even though The Office changed its location over the years, it was a place that felt not quite like home, but familiar. I could get a free soft drink out of the refrigerator or take a pen and a pad of yellow legal paper out of the supply closet. In the 1990s there was the occasional jacket or sweatshirt or feed cap with the name of one of Dad's companies—Fine Builders, Wilfong Construction, Hamilton-Western Utilities, Trotter Range.

More than the outer shell of any particular building, The Office consisted of the personalities who labored indoors, in The Office itself, and outdoors, in the barn and in the construction company. These employees worked for a family business and were indeed part of Ralph's family. They often stayed for years: Pat for 35 years, J.R., the first construction foreman, for 30 years, Jeff Henson, the accountant and party planner, for 25 years. Roger Zapf, who was my age and became the next construction foreman, began working for Ralph right out of high school. When Ralph died, these people and several others clustered at the back of the viewing room at the funeral home for four hours each night and stood vigil as The Office—and Ralph's unofficial—family while his actual blood family stood at the front of the room and greeted visitors.

Then the life span of The Office came to an end, too. In August 2002, Beau put The Office up for sale; he and Pat moved out in November.

R.I.P. The Office.

HERE COMES
TROUBLE

Here Comes Trouble

"Every good thing that comes
is accompanied by trouble."
— MAXWELL PERKINS[11]

When two vowels go walking,
the first one does the talking,
and says its own name.

That's clear enough.[12]

But what, really, is the name of that silent companion who makes himself invisible? He's hiding, but why? What does he get out of it?

Let's consider something good, like children or grand-children—those sweet young things who are not tainted by too many troublesome beliefs just yet.

We love their open-heartedness. Oh, they are so good for us. When we are in their presence, we too can leave our cares behind and just relish the adventure of Now! when

---

11. Speaking upon being assigned as the editor for Thomas Wolfe.
12. In the word *clear*, for example, two vowels, *e* and *a*, are "walking" together, but only *e* speaks.

sticks become swords or moss and acorns become a fairy's house.

Then they are gone, and we feel bereft, sighing deeply at our loss. We look at that first feeling of love, and fail to notice its silent companion of loss—whether for a day or for many months.

We yearn to be in their presence again, giving no thought at all to the parting that inevitably follows. We don't care one jot for the pain that follows our pleasure. We hopscotch from pleasure to pleasure, failing to notice the silent companion of twinge or ache. We wave that trouble away; we let it remain nameless. I want to marinate in those dear names that I so love.

More, please. Let me have more of the good and none of that troublesome stuff.

What's my predilection? More money? Let's not look at the time and energy it takes nor the people who need to be hired to manage it. (Let's hope they're honest.) More clothes? Let's not consider their expense and upkeep, nor the time it takes to go shopping, nor the laborious decision about what to wear today because I have so many choices.

Maybe I'd like more gardens, more flowers, more veggies. But do I have the time and energy for upkeep and maintenance? Picking a bouquet takes time. Harvesting vegetables takes time.

"Takes time" is one of the code names for trouble. For now, the silent companion comes into focus, and his name is trouble. Trouble hides behind the innocent pleasure that seduces us by saying her own name. "New clothes." "More food." "Just one more drink." Hiding behind those sexy legs sticking out of a slinky dress there is a world of trouble, my friend.

Our minds become troubled, whether they are merely bothered or somewhat sad or full-out furious. Trouble comes in so many different disguises.

We crave the pleasure and pay no attention to the fact that pain will indeed follow. We continue to be surprised every time the silent companion worms its way through our heart-mind. We want happiness and forget the unhappiness that inevitably follows. Dualities always balance each other.

If we could clearly see the approach of that silent companion, trouble, what would we do differently? Welcome the good and the beautiful, the trouble and the sorrow, and watch it flow through our lives, knowing already that this beautiful thing or this troublesome thing will come to an end. And then it's gone, regardless of how we feel or think about it. It comes. It goes. Really, that's all.

Wanting and
Not Wanting

IT'S SHARP, THIS FEELING of unwantedness. I want; they apparently do not want. Dare I say it out loud? They don't want me.

Oh, I've suffered plenty of don't-want-ness over the years and decades. Wanting one thing, not wanting another. Grade-school friends, this one, not that one. Wanting fairness and not wanting unfairness to the point of becoming livid, utterly adamant. Wanting to be popular, but since I wasn't, I decided to want unpopularity.

I wanted to be a cheerleader, but my fellow students didn't elect me. They did elect me to be class treasurer, a job I didn't particularly want. In my twenties and thirties, it was easy to work as a bookkeeper—another job I didn't particularly want.

For a while, in my early thirties, I wanted to be the boss, but after one six-month stint as director of a human services agency, I could see that being the one in charge wasn't my forte.

Much later I became a therapist, but I lacked confidence to carry on into private practice after I left my counseling job at a community mental health service. Just a couple of years ago, I met a therapist who worked for HCRS,[13] and he said, "I love reading your intakes. They are so thorough and so well-written." Indeed, I had enjoyed writing up the initial history-gathering interview with each new client; still, this was an interesting perspective to discover fifteen years later.

Now there's something I want, but life is just not unfolding in that direction. I want to teach a meditation class, but students aren't signing up. As Shinzen Young says, "When the teacher is ready, the students will come." The students are not coming to my classes.

For years, decades really, I wanted a relationship. Boyfriends came and went. I wanted what I didn't have. One morning, at age 40, I gave up. I well and truly gave up. I met Bill that same afternoon.

Oh, I've wanted things from Bill over the years that he isn't or doesn't have. I want him to be a good cook, to be organized, to remember where he put his car keys, his glasses, his wallet, his credit card, his cell phone. It pains me that he spends hours every week looking for these things. But I have come to see that looking for things is how he relates to people. This gives him an excuse to call all the places he's been in the past three days, to go to the Latchis Theater mid-morning to look for his lost hat or wallet or phone. He meets and talks to a lot of people on these quests. I have wanted him to be a different person,

---

13. I worked at Health Care and Rehabilitation Services (HCRS), a community mental-health agency, for four years after doing two eight-month internships with the organization.

but now I just laugh and let him be. He doesn't need my help to live his key-less, card-less, cash-less life.

And you, Cheryl—could you just let yourself be as you are? A teacher with so few students that you cancel first one class and then another and then the day-long retreat that only one person has signed up for.

Let go of the tension between wanting and not wanting, and rest in that slack hammock of what is, listening to the birds, feeling the breeze, and watching life unfold.

Fame

WHEN WE WENT TO see the movie "Quartet" in our small town, everyone in attendance was a gray-haired musician—a singer, an instrumentalist, a chorister. Afterward, I heard several murmurings about *Where is there an old-age home for musicians, anyway?*

The plot centers on a haughty, aging diva (Maggie Smith) who arrives at the old-age home for musicians where her ex-husband lives. The residents are planning a concert fundraiser for the home and ask her to join them. The soprano with the once-soaring voice wonders what her fans will think of her if she puts her aged voice on stage in a quartet from *Rigoletto*. (The other three, including the ex-husband, are already in residence at the home.)

She may have been a brilliant opera star in her day, but she still doesn't realize that fame is evanescent. It really does only last for fifteen seconds or maybe fifteen minutes, then the next thing happens, and we're not the star of the moment anymore.

There's a therapist in Hollywood who calls winning an Oscar a 96-hour thrill. Then you're back to waking up with an aching back and a dry mouth and the phone isn't ringing anymore. The world has moved on.

The diva betrays her egotism by asking what her fans will think of her. Bill, my in-house concert pianist, tells me that if he's nervous, then it's all about him instead of the music. He wants the audience to focus on the music. He strives to express, not to impress.

Several of my meditation teacher friends occasionally mention their nervousness before giving a Dharma talk. Last Sunday, I wondered how it was happening that I was even giving a Dharma talk. A blue Prius was being driven to Solar Hill and then someone, I suppose it was me, got out of the car carrying a laptop. Later the theoretical I sat on a cushion and gave meditation instructions, and still another gave a PowerPoint slide show on Burma. It's a very familiar body wearing familiar clothes. And sometimes a familiar self resides there and gets busy doing all the things she loves to do—like write or organize photos into a coherent story.

But, sometimes, well, it's just a mystery.

EVERY GOOD THING

California Strawberries

THIGH GAP IS WHAT young women aspire to nowadays. A gap between the thighs, just below the crotch, through which you can see daylight, which some women naturally have and some women naturally do not have. What is the purpose of thigh gap? In these days, when women mostly wear pants, I don't think it's for anti-chafing. The gap between the thighs looks like a perfect place for a man to stick his penis. Is that what young women want? To have every man look at them with the idea of sticking his penis between their legs?

What about the 27 million sex slaves who have no choice? Teenage girls and children with penises sticking between their legs, going at it since morning and long into the night with no rest. And their reward is perhaps $1 a week for a candy bar.

We went to hear "Cuatro Corridos"—a modern cantata. Four *corridos*, or ballads, are sung by two so-called Mexican prostitutes, although I would call them sex slaves. A prostitute earns money; a sex slave does not. A prostitute has some freedom of movement; a sex slave does not. One *corrido*/ballad was about a woman who went to the village of Tepancingo, Mexico, with promises to take care of the families' daughters. She would take them to the United States, to the land of gold. What the trafficker did not say was that the girls would service the illegal migrants in the strawberry fields of California.

Is that what we're paying for when we buy a package of big, fat California strawberries? The farmer, his undocumented migrant pickers, and the sex slaves who service them?

The fourth *corrido*/ballad was sung by the Chicana policewoman who arrests the ring of human traffickers. Her aria/question is "What happens to these girls now?" They too are illegal immigrants who will be shipped back to Mexico. And then what?

Strawberry margarita, anyone?

BEST OF
THE BLOG
2013

The Divine
Emotions

Loving-Kindness

Compassion

Appreciative Joy

Equanimity

An Amaryllis and the
Four Directions

My amaryllis is blooming, with its four wonderful, large flowers facing in the four directions.

If you have lived (or stayed in a hotel) near a mosque, you know that the P.A. system, with its speakers pointed in the four directions, booms out a resonant call to prayer five times a day. No matter which direction you live in, you can hear the call half a mile away. This reminder of our spirituality pervades the entire area around the mosque.

My amaryllis is silent, but it reminds me to send loving-kindness out to the four directions. Just as sound permeates and pervades all the area around the source of the sound, so loving-kindness can and does infuse the entire area around us. When you're in the presence of a peaceful person or a kind person, you can sometimes feel that calm or kindness permeating *you*.

As the Buddha said,

I will abide pervading one-quarter[14] with a mind
imbued with loving-kindness,
Likewise the second,[15] likewise the third, likewise
the fourth.
So above and below, around and everywhere, and
to all as to myself.
I will abide pervading the all-encompassing world
with a mind imbued with loving-kindness,
Abundant, exalted, immeasurable,
without hostility, and without ill-will.

---

14. That is, one-quarter of the universe (I think of this as one of the
cardinal directions—north, south, east, or west).

15. The second quarter (I think of this as the next cardinal direction).

EVERY GOOD THING

Clogged Openness

Our three-week-old Christmas tree hasn't lost any needles yet. My sweetie has been watering the tree with boiling water. The other day, the tree drank almost the entire tea kettle. Supposedly, boiling water melts the resin that clogs the pores in the stump. The 91-year-old neighbor who taught us this trick said her tree sprouts new growth in *February*.

What clogs up our own openness? We try to protect our feelings, our hearts, and our sense of self. We each have our own methods—irritation, anxiety, denial, and many others.

We can warm up our heart, perhaps simply by placing our hand on our heart. "Yes, yes. There, there, now." Our heart melts, and we too can have the resilience of new (personal) growth.

Wild Food for Wild Women

In early May, my women's group came over for lunch and a tour of my garden, so I served a wild lunch to these wild women: stir-fried fiddleheads, wild leek miso soup, and roasted Jerusalem artichokes. Fritze brought sorrel and nettles. (Oh, I love nettle soup.)

Every woman in this group is on a different spiritual path from each of the others—I'm the only Buddhist, Deb is a Congregational minister, Josephine is a yoga teacher with a strong affinity for Hinduism, Sam is a nonpracticing Jew, Barbara is earth-based, and Fritze refuses any and all categories.

Nevertheless, we've been together for nineteen years, and we love each other. You could even say we're wild about each other.

Johnny-Jump-Ups
as a Cover Crop

The purpose of a cover crop is to increase the fertility of the soil, to decrease weeds and pests, and to create biodiversity. Cover crops are called "green manure" because farmers plow these nitrogen-rich crops into the ground, where they improve the soil.

Most cover crops are in the legume family (alfalfa, vetch, clover) or in the grasses family (rye, oats, wheat, or buck-wheat), but they also include mustard and arugula of the *Brassica* family.

Every spring, my vegetable garden and the nearby strip beds are covered in Johnny-jump-ups (Jjus). They're cute, and to me, they're a weed. But now I've decided I'm using Johnny-jump-ups as my cover crop. Here's why:

- Jjus don't prevent weeds exactly, but each plant covers half a square foot, and nothing grows in the shade of a Jju.

- They bloom profusely in April and May and are a joy to behold.

- In late June they become leggy, so I pull them out wholesale.

- One compost bin is completely full of Jjus. Although they don't fix nitrogen, they're adding a lot of "green manure" to my compost bins.

This is a win-win situation. Beautiful flowering beds in April and May and an overflowing green compost bin in June to really get that compost working.

By the age we are now, we have learned innumerable ways to cover up our authentic selves. Psychologists call these strategies "defense mechanisms," and some of them are quite cute and socially acceptable. For women, one common strategy is self-sacrifice—being sensitive to others' pain and tending to hide our own needs so that we're not a bother. That's our cover crop.

One of these days, it will be time to compost that strategy and practice more kindness toward ourselves. Acting from this base of kindness, we can truly be of service to others.

Glad for Glads

Gladiolas are blooming, and I am glad. I love my glads, which do require the maintenance of digging up the corms in the fall and replanting them in the spring.

Gladness is one of the divine emotions, closely related to loving-kindness. Feeling glad to see a friend is a shout-out of love.

I'm glad to see my old friends, the gladiolas.

Growing Quietly Underground

I love cold-weather crops. In November, garlic is growing in the garden. How delightful and how rare to see small green shoots in the November days of early dark. Garlic isn't the only bulb that's sprouting; the onions that escaped the hide-and-seek of harvest are also sending up green shoots. Now that they've revealed their hiding places, I may pluck them any time for a soup or a stir-fry.

Many other bulbs are growing quietly underground. In fact, we gardeners may even be planting some—daffodils, snowdrops, or squill.

As we enter the darkest quarter of the year (October 31 to February 2), what is growing underground in your heart? Perhaps it's time to practice self-compassion.

For some of us, the outer darkness is reflected by an inner darkness, an inner heaviness or feeling of blah. Winter is the time to practice the equanimity of "Hello, my old friend Blah." Invite Blah and her heaviness in for a cup of tea, and just listen to what she has to say. You don't have to believe every word she says. Simply be a good friend. Be a good friend to yourself.

Crunchy Jerusalem
Artichokes

I did it! I popped a raw Jerusalem artichoke into my mouth and chewed. The flavor is ever-so-slightly sweet, and the crunch—like a water chestnut—is fun. I get busy and make raw kale / raw Jerusalem artichoke salad.

Sometimes we prefer to hear the Buddha's teachings as they've been "cooked" by popular teachers. Sometimes we're ready to read the "raw" words straight from the scriptures of the Pali Canon. The phrase I've been crunching on this week before elections comes from the Buddha's list of improper topics of conversation (for monks, anyway). The list begins, "Kings, robbers, ministers of state . . ." It doesn't take much to translate that into "Presidents, lobbyists, and Congress" or "Presidents, white-collar crime, Wall Street, super PACs, and international affairs."

During election week, it's hard to refrain from all the juicy news, so I limit my intake. Yes, friends bend my ear with their political views. (Are any of these instances of Wise View?) I listen to their fear, their anger, their relief.

Pre-election week is an excellent opportunity to practice compassion—for everyone.

The Winter Garden

In mid-November, the winter vegetable garden still abounds with bok choy, kale, mustard greens, arugula, parsnips, and leeks. In the basement, in storage, are butternut squash, onions, garlic, tomatillos, and Jerusalem artichokes.

The winter of our lives is still fresh for the harvest of wisdom. No longer are we hot tomatoes. Now, with equanimity, born of seeing things as they really are, seeing life as it really is, we can be cool as cucumbers and relax into the unfolding of life. Precious life.

A Poinsettia Reblooms

My poinsettia started blooming in mid-November. What fun to watch the resurrection of last year's plant.

I repotted the poinsettia last spring. Just as I suspected, the roots were bound into a very small peat pot, used for starting seedlings, that had not quite biodegraded. I broke the peat pot open and spread the roots into potting soil in a slightly larger plastic pot than the one I was taking it out of.

From previous experience of trying to keep poinsettias over the summer, there comes a time in April or May when the plant wilts and looks beyond help. Eventually, I discovered that the roots were constrained by a tiny peat pot into a two-inch ball, even though the plastic pot was much larger.

How do we constrain ourselves? What keeps us tightly knotted and prevents us from living our authentic lives? Self-judgment, self-pity, self-isolation, self-absorption are some of the familiar ways of getting locked into the small world of our own thoughts.

Let's tend and befriend ourselves by applying some loving-kindness and compassion to ourselves. Starting with ourselves is not selfish; as conventional wisdom says, we can't love someone else until we love ourselves.

Spread out your roots in your own life, so that you can bloom—even in the winter.

CHERYL WILFONG

Birdhouse Gourds

Last summer, the birdhouse gourd vines covered everything in their path. These vines crawled over nearby shrubs and continued into the lawn for 30 feet. I harvested a couple dozen of these gourds that are so excellent for making birdhouses, and gave many away. The remaining dozen I stored in the basement. I thought it would take six months for them to dry out, but three months later you could hear the seeds rattling inside if you shook them.

Some friends came over in December, and with a drill and three sizes of drill bits, we made our individual birdhouses. The one-inch-wide drill bit makes an opening just big enough for a wren (but not a house sparrow).

In the holiday season, busy-ness runs amok in our lives. What can we harvest from this tangle?

The Divine Abodes are the Buddhist beatitudes:—loving-kindness, compassion, appreciative joy, and equanimity. These divine emotions are the homes where our hearts can dwell and sing songs of joy, just as sweetly as a wren singing its heart out.

Let's make space in our lives for these heavenly houses of kindness, compassion, joy, and peace—the protected spaces we can dwell in.

EVERY GOOD THING

THE SURPRISE
OF MY LIFE

Pray

WHEN I BOUGHT THE land where I live, I found a pile of bricks in the woods. What, pray tell, were they doing there? There weren't that many bricks, fewer than a hundred. Not enough for a big project like a chimney or even a sidewalk. Perhaps the beginning of a project?

The word embossed on each brick said, "PRAY," as if this heavenly order could be set into bricks and mortar and built into some hallowed structure. Perhaps I could build a little stupa—a Buddhist monument, usually roundish like a beehive with a relic of an awakened person hidden inside it.

I've seen those PRAY bricks in a path through the tiny garden of the church in Westminster. So I assume that somewhere around here in Windham County, maybe in Putney, lived a brick maker whose last name was Pray.

I teach a meditation class in Springfield on Tuesday nights, and a Baptist who once attended said, "I'm not going to pray to the Buddha." I heartily agreed with him. "I'm not praying to the Buddha, either," I said, "since he is not a god and certainly *not* a grantor of desires."

When I'm introducing mindfulness to an ecumenical audience, I tell them about Mother Teresa's definition of "pray." In a 1986 interview, Dan Rather asked her what she said when she prayed.

"Oh, I don't say anything," she replied. "I listen."

"And what does God say?" Dan Rather asked.

"Oh, he doesn't say anything either. He's listening too."

Listening to stillness is such an excellent form of prayer. One 93-year-old meditation student told me that her favorite word is "tranquility." Very hard of hearing, she loved listening to the sound of silence. After I led her through a loving-kindness meditation, I asked her what she thought of sending loving-kindness to someone you hold a grudge against.

"Oh, I love everyone equally," she said. "It's a great grace."

She, who had prayed the rosary for so many decades, eventually stumbled into the daily divine, and now she was content to sit in the tranquility of stillness and simply listen.

Dying Hundreds of Times

IF I BELIEVE I was born, then, of course, I must die. Birth is followed by death.

But wait a minute. Is that infant swaddled in a blanket really me? I've been told that it was me. The little girl in a plaid dress tied into a bow at the back: they said that was five-year-old Cheryl. My name is Cheryl. I remember that place where the photo was taken. Therefore that must be me.

But really, that belief is just a thought happening in the present moment. Perhaps an evocative thought with love and nostalgia all mixed up with it. And those emotions are happening in the present moment, too. I can never touch the past, nor the future, either. That little girl is long gone, never to be seen again. The past is a thought. It's just a thought. The future is a thought. It's just a thought. Take a look and see for yourself.

This leaves me with the present moment, into which I am continually born and continually dying. Every moment is my last moment. What more could I wish for than to be here where I am? Desiring something is useless. Think about it.

Oh! There's a phone call I "need" to make. But I'm not making it now. The phone is across the room or in my pocket. Near or far, "phone call" is just an idea that is making me up. *Oh! I need to buy something for dinner tonight.* I'm not at the store. Nor am I at dinner. Dinner is just another thought. Shopping is still another thought that I want to cling to tightly so that the *I* I've made up won't forget it.

If I narrow my focus to this moment of moving a blue pen across blue lines on a sheet of paper, where is my birth and where is my death? Each letter is born onto paper, born into words, sentences, paragraphs, then gone, forgotten. I don't even know what word I wrote 30 seconds ago. It has died, as has the self that wrote it.

What if I am not born? No birth, no death. No self, no problem. The words flow onto paper. A body sits in a chair. Awareness sees/feels/hears this happening. But where is the *I*?

Oh yes, I have a ton of *I*'s stockpiled for use. Habits of self that I can feel into and out of faster than you can say Jack Robinson. The writer self. The listening self. The reading self. The knitting self. The self does something, says something, then it dies. Here we are, sitting quietly, listening to someone read. Actually, vibrations are striking our eardrums. That is all.

We listen to our internal commentary, or the mind drifts away to another self. Then the reading self ends. We could say it dies. A speaking self is born and then dies. So many births and deaths in one day, one hour, one minute. It's enough to make you dizzy.

Just give me some inner stability in the sea of life. So I reach for the grip of the *I*, and I hold on. And this *I* puts me in the precarious position of being born and therefore dying.

EVERY GOOD THING

Would you prefer one conundrum over the other? No matter. The moment is gone. Rest in peace, O Writing-Self who has ten more minutes to live. Life is short. Clutch the blue pen to make it do your will. The blue pen is your staff of life, the thing that creates a self. When Jan, our writing group's leader, rings the bell, that self dies. Writing stops. Talking begins. We are born and we die hundreds of times a day, but it's so much easier not to notice, so much easier to ignore death, pretend it isn't there. So much easier and more fun, too, to believe the story of past and future and just ignore this ever-changing moment that is life.

So the minutes, hours, and days go on, one after the other. Our death hiding in every single one of them.

The Garden of Eden

SHE DISCOVERED THAT THE Garden of Eden is right here, right now, but the people around her failed to notice. They were too busy living in their minds instead of their hearts. They were too busy believing every story the mind told them. She knew this, because it happened to her, too.

"I have to make that phone call." "Send that e-mail." "I've got to arrange for this." "I have to go shopping for dinner." "I need to lose weight." "I should exercise." Et cetera. Et cetera.

We're too busy living in the virtual reality of past and future. "What will they think of me?" If I don't do what others are doing, what will they think of me? If I wear bright turquoise pants to the wedding, what will people say? Et cetera. Et cetera.

Most people don't realize that the Garden of Eden is all around them. We're too busy pronouncing judgments. Sorting the world into good and bad, right and wrong, black and white, proper and the can-you-believe-it, look-down-your-nose impropriety that is just begging for a sarcastic remark.

Rest your eyes and see the Garden of Eden right here, right now. If you like, you can feel God strolling here in the cool of the evening, but it doesn't have to be God. We could call it Life. Life walking all around the Tree of Life, passing right by the Tree of the Knowledge of Good and Evil, that black-and-white, good-and-bad, right-and-wrong tree where Life is separated into me and you, us and them, even I and Thou.

The Tree of Life calls us to sit under its wide-spreading branches. Rest here and look at Life looking at Life. Rest from your gardening of the world. Rest from organizing other people's lives. Rest from minding other people's business. Life is just as it is.

Call this just-as-it-is-ness God if you wish. Call the Nameless a name if you must speak of it to others. But for now, sit here in the arboreal Church of the Nameless, church of the self-less, and simply look at Life looking at Life, feel Life feeling Life, or walk with Life walking in Life.

Simply notice the mystery that Life is gardening Life. Separate seeming, yet not separate. Not two, but not the oneness of God, either. Wholeness perhaps. Just-as-it-is-ness perhaps.

Let's go for a walk in the garden now.

Nothing Could Have Surprised Me More

I SPENT THE FIRST FEW days at the meditation retreat following the instructions to note "real" and "unreal," "existent" and "nonexistent."

Now, you might wonder *what's the use of that?* We live in reality, as in "Welcome to the real world, babe," and the material world obviously exists.

But not so fast, my dear. Let's apply our magnifying glass and search or re-search this idea of existence.

The coffee table in front of you, for instance. Normally, we would say, "The coffee table exists." After all, you may be relaxing your feet on it.

But if we took the legs off the coffee table, would it still exist as a coffee table? It could be a very awkward large tray, or perhaps a sled that doesn't slide all that well on the snow. The coffee table has lost its coffee-table-ness.

Going back further in time we can imagine this coffee table as a tree. And going forward in time, it will eventually become firewood. So where's the inherent coffee-table-ness to the coffee table?

You could be picky and say it exists now, but, okay, it didn't use to exist and it won't exist in the future. This drives us back to the definition of "exists." If something doesn't exist, then does, then doesn't, is that what you call "exists"?

You'd think that "exists" must mean something permanent. But are we using "exists" to refer to something that also didn't and won't exist? How existent is that?

You'd think that "existent" means existent and "nonexistent" means nonexistent.

So, unfortunately, we have to throw the coffee table into the nonexistent category, along with coffee mugs, magazines, and everything else on it, as well as the carpet and floor it sits on.

Wait a minute! the mind protests.

But I'm asking you to wait a minute yourself. If we had an electron microscope and looked at the coffee table, we would see nothing but space. There's 500 times as much space as those tiny electrons take up in every atom of the coffee table.

Okay. We can admit that, theoretically, the material world is made up of space, but electrons—they must surely exist.

If there were a physicist here, she could tell us about the composition of an electron. Really, it's just energy moving very fast, blinking into and out of existence (ahem) at a very rapid rate.

In our language, verbs move and nouns refer to things. But nouns aren't as stable as we would like to think. Nouns themselves are simply slow-moving verbs. We can't see the change, we can't see the movement in the coffee table (unless we have a very concentrated mind), so we assign thing-ness to it, and that thing-ness fools us into thinking it's somehow permanent or stable, when actually, my dear, the darn coffee table doesn't even "exist" at all.

So, as you can now imagine, at the retreat I moved around labeling everything as nonexistent, partly as a way to drive it into my pea-brain that the things I think exist don't. Not really.

And that brings us to the subject of "real" and "unreal." We believe we live in the real world. We believe that things such as the coffee table have inherent existence—even though we also thoroughly know (heh heh heh) that we've never seen a coffee table exactly like this one. What we "know" is the category "coffee table." We've seen thousands of coffee tables, and quite probably they've all been different. When we say "category," we're talking about a concept.

Temple Grandin, who is on the autism spectrum, describes this automatic "seeing" in her book *Thinking in Pictures*. When she hears the word dog, she sees a quick slide show in her mind of the thousands of dogs she's ever seen. We do the same thing, but we're not aware of it.

The concept "dog" or "coffee table" is not real. It's a useful category, but it's not reality.

And thoughts. All those dozens of thoughts that zoom through our minds every minute, how real are they? *Psst.* Every thought is unreal, too.

So, on this meditation retreat, after I'd spent three days labeling everything as nonexistent or unreal, and I mean everything, nothing could have surprised me more than Reality revealing itself.

For three days, I peeled off every label; I was mindful of the unreality of thousands of perceptions—thoughts, breath, sensations. Everything coming and going. And

EVERY GOOD THING

all that attention came to fruition one afternoon while I was taking a walk with the tree identification app on my iPhone. Yes, trees are nonexistent and unreal, but still, I was interested in identifying the nine varieties of oaks there in the Virginia woods.

I had just labeled the white swamp oak when I realized that the trees were seeing me even though I thought I was looking at them. Not only the trees. The sky, the ground, and the very air were alive and looking. Life was looking at Life. No me. No them. No things at all. No things to be interconnected. Only Life changing and shifting from moment to moment.

The familiar thing I call I dropped to her knees in the woods, just sitting, smiling, and watching the surprise we call life.

CONCLUSION

Death Talk

"WHY DO YOU ALWAYS talk about death?" a 35-year-old mother of young children asks me. I've noticed that 30-somethings don't like the idea of death.

A few years ago, my friend Joan and I had lunch every other Wednesday to do what Joan called our "terminal papers." We planned our funerals. Joan was 72 and her husband, Ed, had already survived a car accident that left him in a coma for five weeks. Afterward he couldn't finish writing the physics textbooks he'd been working on. Then a couple of years later the doctor accidentally discovered Ed had pancreatic cancer. A quick operation and Ed was saved again. It took another couple of years for Ed to really hold his own in ordinary conversation. A year later something else went wrong. Was it liver cancer? No, it didn't seem to be. He just became weaker and weaker.

But back to Joan's and my terminal papers. We discussed funeral homes, cremations, music, songs, our obituaries, and people who might be of assistance.

Joan wanted me to meet her 40-year-old daughter. Joan reviewed her funeral plans, and her daughter burst into tears. "Stop talking to me about this. Just get it done. I can't take it."

I recognized this feeling. Every time Bill mentions death—says, for instance, that he's already lived longer than his older brother did—his daughter says, "Oh, you're healthy. You're going to live a long time."

Our 52-year-old neighbor had the stamina of a horse and gave colon cancer and the metastasized liver cancer a good long run. He played soccer every week for two years after his diagnosis, all through his chemotherapy, but eventually death overpowered his will to live.

I tried to explain my interest in death to my middle-aged friend. I told her that I'm trying to prepare for it now by developing good habits of the mind. I'm trying to root out some of the weeds of anger and fear. What happens if we see some nightmare vision when we've crossed to the other side? What happens if we glimpse a hell realm? I want to respond with compassion toward those who are burning with their suffering, which means I have to start developing that habit now. Avoiding scary situations now is like refusing to exercise, refusing to take a walk. I want to learn to meet fear. I want to get to know it well, so that I'll have that strength if I need it later on.

I told her, "I guess I believe that you're not fully living unless you've faced the fact of dying."

"Yeah," she said. "But do you have to talk about it so much?"

Good question.

The Certainty of Uncertainty

MY NEIGHBOR WHIT WAS at the gym one Friday morning in April when his heart stopped. Fortunately, Supreme Fitness had a defibrillator, and the staff knew how to use it. It's battery-powered, and it won't work if there is a pulse. They laid it onto his chest, and the message said, "Prepare to shock."

Whit thought he had fainted, and he was ready to go home. "Not so fast," said the cardiologist who sent him up to Dartmouth-Hitchcock Hospital.

The mind seeks an explanation and tries desperately to concoct a story. Whit is a homebody who spends most of his days alone, since his 70-year-old wife has gone back to work this year. Most days he goes to the Putney Food Co-op for lunch.

Two months earlier, in February, we were traveling together in Laos. One month earlier, he was traveling alone in Egypt. If his heart had stopped at home, perhaps at the co-op, or definitely in Laos or Egypt, I'd be going to a funeral today.

Instead, Whit had triple bypass surgery three days later. His grandchildren, whom he had visited in England three weeks earlier, still have a grandfather.

The mind boggles. It simply cannot figure out this turn

of events. Emotions range from deep gratitude to fear that another shoe will drop.

One by one, my peers are afflicted with chronic diseases. Life is uncertain. I feel I'm skating on thin ice myself. When will the ice crack? I wonder. Because that's one thing I am sure of: the ice will crack and break. Suddenly or slowly. I don't know. I would say the suspense is killing me, but that's a little too close to the mark.

Uncertainty is the only thing I can be certain of.

I Won't Live Forever

MY NEIGHBOR'S HEART STOPPED while he was exercising at the gym. Fortunately, they had a defibrillator, and the trainer had been a medic in Iraq, so Whit is living longer than he would have otherwise.

Meanwhile, Kathy, who had stood at the cash register at Brown & Roberts Hardware Store for 31 years, is dead. She bled to death on the operating table even though she was surrounded by the utmost in medical equipment and technicians.

The Dalai Lama says, "We don't know what will come first: rebirth or tomorrow."

Just in case I don't make it past tomorrow, what is it finally time to do?

I am acting as if my timeline is somewhat longer, and so I am planning to offer a retreat in July. Otherwise, today is a good day of writing, doing The Work, yoga, and meditation. Even the trip to Bellows Falls this afternoon to look at a retreat center will be okay, because I'll stop at the Allen Brothers and Harlow's farm stands, and the Agway farm and garden center in Walpole.

It is time to do my monthlong retreat this year. But not yet. May is for gardening, and it's time to spend my energy on that work of great impermanence. If I died in my garden, anyone's garden really, I would be content.

It turns out that I don't have time to "finally have time" until four months from now.

Today it's time to watch a bee crawling on a dandelion, listen to a crow cawing, feel the sun's heat on my forearm while the star magnolia flowers begin to brown at the ends of their floppy white petals, which float to the brown earth. They don't live forever.

Set Me Out in the Garden

Set me out in the garden, no matter the weather, no matter whether there even is a garden. Set me on a bench, even if I slump to one side. I would love a glider, but failing that, prop me up against a tree.

If it's a November day, like the November fifth when my dad died at dawn, lean me up against a tree so I can feel the bite of the wind on my cheeks. I recently saw a photo of a baby in Lapland fast asleep leaning against a recumbent white reindeer. The heavily padded baby had black hair and rose-red cheeks. Set me there next to him so I can bask in the sunny day or the moonlit night.

Let me lose my individual sense of self as I melt into the earth and trees. You will see an old lady dying and will want to rush in to make me comfortable, to alleviate your own fear of the dark and the cold. But I will be seeing something else, the unrolling unfolding of Life. Let it be, just as it is.

Perhaps it will be an early summer day like the day I found a chipmunk asleep under the leaves of a violet. No, not asleep. Dead. Head resting on forepaws.

Lay me down in the garden so that I may rest on the earth until I can no longer differentiate between the solidity of earth and the solidity of body—the body becoming part of earth. No difference.

Let me disappear into twinkling lights in space.

CHERYL WILFONG

Reading *The Tibetan Book of the Dead*

A
FTER MY HOSPICE CLIENT died in January, I began reading *The Tibetan Book of the Dead* to her, just in case the dead can actually hear what we say to them, as the Tibetans claim. After all, the actual name of the book is *The Great Liberation Through Hearing in the Between.*

I'm always a bit wary of reading Tibetan scriptures to a Christian. What will the dead Christian think of all those Buddhas and their consorts? Even I think they're grisly, what with skull bowls and drinking blood and so forth. But the overall message makes intuitive sense to me. Perhaps the soul does wander around in the days after the body dies. In that dream world between death and whatever happens next, the disembodied might be tempted by various visions, so these instructions are meant to guide them safely to the Lord of Great Compassion.

During the first seven days, the instructions are clear: Go toward the blindingly bright lights, every day a different color, and avoid those very tempting smoky lights, also a different color every day, that will lead the spirit right back onto the wheel of samsara.[16] Sort of like landing on a chute in the game of Chutes and Ladders, where you fall right back into incarnation in some realm—animal or human, godly or ghostly. All the realms are time-limited. Even the god realms only last a mere 84,000 years. When you look around, you see this could be true. The Greek gods and the Norse gods are dead. And Yahweh is a mere 6,000 years old, not even as old as some of those Hindu gods and goddesses.

So if you don't want to be reborn into this samsaric existence, head toward the bright light. But on the eighth day, the game gets serious. The visions become terrifying in an effort to scare you into the seeing the clear light of the mind.

The first time I read *The Tibetan Book of the Dead*, when I was 28, I had to stop because I was having nightmares of zombies cooking bodies in aluminum foil, like so many hot potatoes.

When I'm reading all this imagery to the deceased, I translate it into terms I think a Christian might understand: Bodhisattvas become saints, devas become angels, and the Buddha, well, let's just leave that as the vague title "Lord." We won't get specific about which one.

After I'd been reading to my deceased hospice client for three weeks, I was concerned that I wouldn't finish the 49-day ritual before I left on my month-long retreat.

One afternoon in mid-February, as I was sitting in the hot tub, a rainbow off to the northeast surprised me. A

---

16. Samsara is the endless series of births and deaths to which all beings are subjected.

rainbow? In February? When was the last time you saw a rainbow in the snow? When I sat down to read *The Book of the Dead*, the instruction for the day was to recognize the rainbow body. I took that to mean that I had received a sign: my hospice client had reached her after-death home and had no further need of instruction from me.

And when, two months later, I received a request to write a magazine article about my work as a hospice volunteer, I was sure it was her way of winking at me and saying *Thank you.*

CPSIA information can be obtained at www.ICGtesting.com
Printed in the USA
LVOW06s1307161213

365528LV00002B/2/P

9 780982 566459